for,

the Link
secondary
school @
beddington.

~ *emptiness fills me* ~

enjoy !

Antony

4/12/17
x

~ emptiness fills me ~

~ siafu unframed ~

~ Antony Lipski ~

'emptiness fills me,
being one with emptiness,
emptiness fills me . . .'

~*~

To order additional copies of this book, contact:
Xlibris Corporation
0-800-644-6988
www.xlibrispublishing.co.uk
orders@xlibrispublishing.co.uk
300108

Contents

~ PART I: ~ Poetry ~

• zen/meditation

• autobiography

• nature

• to loved ones/friends

• potpourri

~ PART II: Prose ~

• travelogues

• zen reflections

• memoir

• philosophical reflection

~ epilogue ~

*

it is not enough to speak and write well,
nor enough to be seen to be
doing the right thing.

it is only enough
when life IS justly discharged
in the light and action of truth.

when nobody sees, and no one knows—
a cloak of invisibility obscures rightful deeds
performed in the right way
simply because: that IS the way to be.

I vow, therefore,
never to write another word
which seeks to redeem me
without aspiration to live a nobler life.

too often the word is disaffected in the deed,
vouchsafe, not another phrase will escape my pen,
save to countenance a thought
that is practiced in endeavour
and realized in accomplishment.

~*~

author's preface

This book began life as a daily blog on an internet social networking site in August 2006. I found, to my great wonder and encouragement that my poetry, myriad reflections and observations had gained a fairly wide, enthusiastic and increasingly devoted following from readers dotted around the globe ~ many people responded, especially a number of close friends, commenting on the inspirational nature of my writing. This recognition correspondingly fuelled me to continue writing and over the course of the next three years, I found myself creating entries, virtually daily, both in prose and poetic form.

My 'world outlook' has been deeply influenced and determined by my belief and faith in Soto Zen Buddhism, as will become evident. It became challenging to categorise the following material, but I have broken down what follows into the subsequent groupings:

PART I:

Poetry:

- zen/meditation
- autobiography
- nature
- loved ones/friends
- potpourri

PART II:

Prose:

- travelogue
- zen reflection

- memoir
- philosophical reflection

- epilogue: *siafu unframed*

PART I

~ Poetry ~

• *zen/meditation*

one attachment

there being one attachment
and one only that I
cherish,

'tis to rush, headlong
into the moment,
THIS moment.

oh beauty! diving deeply,
an endless vista of intimacy.

silence beholding myriad song,
blood sibilating through
enlightened frame,
sighing sweet
harmony.

gentle hum of the city,
wind nestling in the trees,
the fragile light of autumn
pixillating across a
beneficent universe.

emergent realisation!

bliss, warmth
and harmony.

plateau reached,
the bell strikes
twice.

coming home

on
returning
unceasingly
into silence
is our refuge
our true home,
our resting place.

wherever
breath takes place,
therein stillness.

therein the
joy of Being,
eternally.
here,
now.

as I sat

as I sat
this morning,
opening, letting go,
dissolving experience,
sitting still amidst the chaos,
inconsistencies and unknowns,
confusion of understanding.

all at once,
the storm abated.
relinquishing fear,
the need to *know*,
the need to control,
the need to *be in* control.

trusting in the simplest of processes,
of breathing and being.

Truth dawned upon me
in all Its majesty.

the joy of Being arose as a well spring,
a dance of luminescence.

the blossoming of peaceful
contentment and gratitude
for This, just as It is,
bright, unadorned
consciousness,
as I sat.

celebrating This

now!
the distant roar of awakening
tumbles through my imagination,
ambrosial waterfall,

joyfully cascading 'twixt thoughts
of splendid freedom from anxiety and fear,
ambiguity recedes into the distance.

teasingly,
as scudding clouds
weave their erratic and mindless
path 'cross pastel sky,
does my reasoning mind
lie dormant at the feet of Immediacy.

tantalizingly,
peaceful Presence erases barriers
to the truth of this moment,
caressing me bounteously
'midst flexible breath.

throwing myself
into this mix with pure
unadulterated abandon,
glorying in the vagaries
of timeless meandering,

somewhat as the course
of a country river, snaking through
spongy meadows,
absorbing nectarine perfume
from all manner of
gaily coloured
vegetation.

meanwhile, rain courses
bountifully, horizontally, outside
in the cold dark night
that is winter.

the contrast is not lost on me;
privilege sits squarely 'pon shoulders
risen from fractured soil,
to face this wondrous moment,
head bowed in thanksgiving.

in gratitude

ahh!
this morning
as I sat, diving deep
into Eternal's embrace,
I basked in total Absorption.

the warmth and intimacy
of all received memory,
feeling and presence
staggered me
in their intensity.

true connection with Life,
groundedness and exemplary attunement
with every scrape of experience
of a life lived in all its fullness,
fortune, misfortune, luck,
melancholy.

I no longer want for anything
but bask daily in great fortune
that was, is and will be my lot,
despite the inevitability
of the soul's eventual
passing,

all is well.

with bows

aum

sitting
very still.

escaping the confines
of little self.

a
perceptible shift in
awareness.

breathing in the history
of the universe.

breathing out,
consciousness
cascading faultlessly
into the vault
of eternity,

nothing lost,

a gaining of
boundless
merit.

on getting nowhere

returning
to the moment is,
simply the only way to travel,
coming back ~ to *this*.

travelling daily
out into the world,
effortlessly caught up in
the fantasies of our social persona.

so caught up in these imaginings
as to be emotionally snagged
into believing what
we feel is real,
is the truth.

and yet that
still small voice
ne'er satisfied.

striving for that extra piece
of the puzzle that will
make it all
okay.

my advice ~
give it up,
get up with it!

let go of cherished constructs
of stability and permanence,

throw yourself into the abode
of emptiness and unknowing,
for therein lies the key
to wisdom, compassion
and tranquility.

returning to the moment
is simply the only way
to travel.

coming back ~ to *this*.

try it.

delving deeply into 'I'

contrary
to most journeys,
the travel inwards begins
with no movement,
absolute stillness.

as the ability to hold still manifests,
a swelling unfolds, invisibly growing,
until it embraces all, everything.

centre becomes eclipsed by periphery,
margins divide seamlessly into the whole,
no comings or goings, to-ings or fro-ings
just open to breath.

with the purity of being
'I' shines brightly, undimmed divinity
beyond the power of expression
and thought.

welcome home.

that still, small voice

that ubiquitous, indefinable
still small voice,

the more that you
struggle to hear It,
most elusive
does it become,

and yet this
modest companion
is our foundation,
our salvation,

our succour in times
of inchoate delusion.

without conscious
apprehension,
upon its Truth
do we depend.

delighting in obscurity,
dependent for recognition
solely upon our
faith, silence, stillness and humility,

that ubiquitous, indefinable
still small voice,

the more that you
struggle to hear It,
most elusive does it become.

each day

each day
brings us closer.
each day we strive for
a better way of apprehending
our circumstance.

yet our yearning is
tinged with no little fear
and a measure of despair.
for realisation brings with it
a taste of our mortality.

however,
with patience and determination
we may discover hidden truths,
untouched landscapes of inner perfection
and timelessness.

the quieter we become, the stiller we sit,
the more able to relinquish,
the greater the peace,
the stronger the joy,
the clearer the inner space,
allowing us complete and unbound freedom.

breath opened up to ~ hope dissolves into
unreserved acceptance of boundless fortune
and the wondrous luck at being,
here ~ now.

awake, aware, able
to apprehend, taste, feel,
immerse ourselves in
the ambrosia of our form,
yet intrinsic formlessness,
but we have
the courage
to face
IT

betwixt and between

is it we, or the world
that is filled with hope?
is it us, or the world
that lives in despair?

peering through our shadowed frame,
is love radiating
or merely pain?

eternal wanderings back and forth;
rarely settled—Truth
or merely solace?

gentle sun filters silent golden rays
through multi-layered shades of
natural colour;

mesmerizing thought . . .
is it within or without?

wondering why
with child-like eye,
eternal fascination,
gaze turned to sky.

never too late to chase dreams
of peace and redemption.

thanking powers that be for the
grace of Awareness
and the facility of silent gratitude.

unanswerable questions
litter my path, lighten my load,
through mysterious open-ended Presence,
insights unfold.

of which all is part

the search for peace continues unabated,
yet there is no such thing, there is only holding,
like the most delicate, precious Ming vase,
this apprehension that is our very birthright.

to appreciate this jewel
is not easy at the best of times

to accept This ~ as It is,
unadorned, unvarnished,
the dirt, the mess the excrement.
all is part, all is part.

the violence, the inequality,
the folly of catastrophe
all is part, all is part.

I learn not to judge,
neither to discriminate
to be open, to be compassionate,

to be okay with This,
and that which I fear,
which I do not understand.

the search for peace continues unabated,
yet there is no such thing, there is only holding,
like the most delicate, precious Ming vase,
this apprehension that is our very birthright.

just a thought

oh! let me dig deep,
allow me to find Truth
within the most menial
of chores,

for who would not,
upon viewing a panorama
of conventional beauty,
be driven to ecstasy and thrill?

but who, if truth be told, surrenders 'will'
when, on hands and knees,
scrubbing dirt from soiled floor,
is thus equally transported?

now—this is my task—

to give of myself wholly, completely
to every machination of the daily round,
discriminating not
'twixt sacred and mundane.

standing: cold, wet,
filthy grey, nauseous,
urban decay beheld—
nothing on the face of it
to feel good about, and yet,

opening to that moment,
was indeed transported by the beauty
within the desolation and decay.

long may I feel open to all moments—
good, bad, and especially, indifferent!

die-v-in

diving
into the moment,

with soundless splash,
the universe opens unto me,
spontaneously my body melts,
as sand running through an hourglass.

thought touching
each existential strand,
intense peace abounds,
silently reverberating across
boundless galaxies.

I love being
here, there, everywhere,
the ripples of my smile
cascade like mountain ranges
across the emptiness
that fills all space.

dieing happily at each moment,
to be reborn—instantly—
again and again
and again,

diving
into the moment.

arising

21ˢᵗ March

today,
a special day
in celebration of
a remarkable event.

t'was on this turning point
many years ago that I chanced
to visit the very spot in lumbini grove,
whence queen maya gave birth to
that north indian prince whose
insights changed, change
and will change
so many lives.

sitting beneath the very tree
of his definitive arrival to these parts,
I grew into my life
and have never since
looked back.

pain and the fear simply
coalesced into faith and a
determination to root out
insecurities, favour the ephemeral
and rejoice in the transient nature
of existence.

I bow with gratitude to
the good fortune of my
late awakening.

*'pon the withered tree
a bud blooms.'*

beatitude

oh glorious early morning, suffused in calm euphoria,
how blessed indeed to inhale perfumed honeyed ethereal prajna,
engaged, throwing open the blessed limbs of creation,
unraveling the night's mysteries and disgorging fear, fantasy and disquiet
in delightful abandon,

secure in the knowing, firm, grounded in the faith of eternal peace,
nothing and no-one can harm you, for there is none there to touch,
the delicate subtle and even-toned atmosphere envelops abiding
consciousness and allows true expression of wonder delight and joy,

nothing there, I repeat—nothing there,
nowhere to rest, going nowhere, nothing to fear,
nowhere is indeed everywhere in this realm of comprehension,
and always, returning to the simple, inexorable, uncontaminated breath,

inhaling, exhaling, the breath of life,
inadvertent, ongoing, endless, goal-free,
life and death have neither credence nor import in this realm,
follow your path and let go of It all,

oh glorious early morning where nothing exists
save This.

offering

a pink shadow,
borne gently, tremulously
from wondrous heavenly globe
falls silently across the floor,
in front of my impassive gaze,

separating light from dark.

the brilliant light of understanding
bestrides my undulating mind,
like a wave of compassion.

breaking gently onto the shore of today,
nestling lightly amongst the pebbles of awareness.

creating a pool of delight
and open-ended expectation,

heralding a new dawn.
an unexpected, unbidden
sense of gratitude
blows through
the window of my soul.

rustling the wide opened curtains
of conscience and awe.

listening

heart, heart is all.

to give of your all—
give all your heart.

it is not possible
to find censure
in the openness
of sincerity.

the declaration, honesty
and legitimacy
of wholehearted passion,

to find yourself is
to forget yourself.

to give of yourself,
we are asked no more than this.

follow the dictates
of your heart,

and no one, nothing
could possibly separate
you from Truth.

so unlike Canute

fragile shell of contradiction,
abstractedly surveying the
breathless rush of Circumstance
that evolves unceasingly before our gaze.

unable to take pause ~ willing a break,
a separation, simply to allow
recollection and reflection to take root
and establish a sense of belonging.

alas! like said sad king,
unable to withstand the tide,
we, forlorn, must abandon all attempts
at control and manipulation.

lo! within despair,
surrender holds the eternal secret,
such sweet transformation sits patiently
at the gateless gate of acceptance.

ruthless flow that supplies
form and substance to our vision.

unlike Canute, we may choose to
bow to the onrush of inevitability,
develop humility and wisdom in
the face of this merciful
act of contrition.

happily the salt sweet
waves of reality envelop us,
and we are able to submerge into
an ocean of sensibility without rancour.

accepting all, we are swept along the eternal route
to an unimaginable future of wonder and completion,
royal road abdicated in the face of our humanity.

the humble mat

lo! nothing seems to matter much
'cept the 'here and now,'
'tis all the merest fleeting glimpse,
is all the gods allow.

alas! it all becomes too much
for fevered mind to grasp
I'll wager all my garnered sense—
these feelings, they will pass.

awakening achieved on humble mat,
my heart doth open wide,
my thanks to You for showing me,
impeccable earthly guide.

sitting still on humble mat
doth appease my febrile brow,
why! bless you Lord for showing me
the Way, the Truth,

the Present ~ here and now.

in remembrance of things to come

maybe ~ just maybe
I'm getting it right.

lately yes!
lately ~ developing insight,

endlessly spiraling heavenward,
sweating out the good,
bad and misunderstood.

faithfully, boundlessly, tirelessly
embroidering gratitude
into a daily callisthenic.

mouthed silent prayers
escape wordlessly,
leaking out constantly
from the open estuary of my soul.

enabled by right physical posture,
true spiritual leanings will shine forth.

perchance to use every
opportunity to bow mindfully,
sow seeds of good practice
minutely, hourly, daily ~
eternally.

surf breathing

it struck me this morning whilst sitting,
the amazing correspondence between breathing
and the rhythm of the surf
at ocean's edge.

indescribable thrill of natural breath
working autonomously,
day in day out,
on and on.

deep satisfaction of the
effortless drawing in of oxygen,
then exhalation of used air,
gently dispelled from frame,
again and again
and again.

how marvelous would it be
if the rhythm of one's breath
was as tranquil as the
ineffable meandering of surf!

imagine if you will,
breathing in as the pull of
thousands of kilometres of water
drags salty foam across the sand,

many moments later,
fresh ripples of foam cascade mightily forward,
breaking laterally along beach's infinite width.

another moment,
another breath,
eternal repose.

lost & found

forever knocking on some door,
to all appearances abandoned,
yet with slightest effort ~ prised apart,
therein amongst the debris,
fecundity abounds!

thoughts

treading lightly on the floorboards of life,
the earth's gentle spin, propelling me forward,
massages my body as impassive divinities
nourish my thoughts.

harmonies radiate through
the chambers of my soul,
as soft west winds
ease across my brow.

gratitude pierces my heart,
murmuring gently
into the channels of
consciousness.

humour, beckoning playfully,
disguises the forces of doubt
which surround the ether
with undetectable aroma.

flirtatious smiles,
masquerading as clouds,
prod me into awakening.

as long as there is breath in me
will I bow to
the bounteous generosity of the Eternal
for Its gracious embrace.

creation

and now
the bubble bursts,
as the fruits of thought
bite the dust and ambiguity takes a stranglehold.

truths,
which appear
in their nature self-evident,
become a graveyard of abused quotations.

knowing
becomes bewilderment
and suspense becomes the order of the day.

fear
grips the soul,
desolation litters the sacraments
a terror of the unknown, unbehest—reigns.

never
is composure regained,
the landscape of sanity vanishes,
an anguished vista of broken hopes prevails.

the dream
is over, the source dries up,
bleakness becomes the order of the day.

amelioration then returns from negative construct,
colour returns, vibrancy becomes a
distinct prospect
again.

the doubt that manifests is seen for what it is,
nature never more apparent and clear,
dawning understanding
once again holds
sway.

broken dreams become a distant echo of thought,
a halo of transcendent beauty
manifests
itself.

reconstruction is underway and breath arises,
the wind escapes confines of
entrapment,
all is
well.

a distant memory of times long cherished
arises from the syrupy soup of
oblivion, whence the
soul breaks
free.

no matter is ever the same again, alas
but redemption is once
again a possibility,
freedom finally
arises from
the

depths of innermost conception and a
universal sigh of relief springs
tempest-like from
the heavens.
~ amen ~

It

within,
all is
still

without,
all is
within

stillness
suffuses
all
existence

within
the
heartbeat,
within
the movement
lies
perfect
stillness

hear it,
listen to
the silence
within

open
body, heart, mind
to
the overwhelming
emptiness
of
Truth

virulent thoughts

loving kindness is like a virus,

beware! hugely contagious,
even known to mend broken hearts,
repair twisted thoughts,
often disguised as happiness.

observe carefully
for subtle signs,
smiles, affection,
hugs and warmth.

however, this deadly affectation
is easily combated,

simply harden your heart,
avoid compassion
and empathy like the plague,
(which will soon return, fear not!)

and soon normal misery will be restored
and life can continue
in glorious grey mode!!

no need to acquiesce;
no need to feel vulnerable
and soft any more.

fear not! it is as easy as sin
to prevent this deadly virus
from penetrating your inner core:

be ever vigilant and watch out for signs
of a shared delight
and the scariest manifestation of all ~

Peace . . .

fridayHaiku

thoughts dissolve,
joys abound . . .

bodily bereft
yet spiritually
crowned . . .

mentally disrobed
tho' inherently sound . . .

memories fade,
the moment
is found!

as It is

holding still—opportunity.
awareness, rising like the sun.

the dawn of understanding
unfolds spontaneously.

life penetrates
every atom of every pore.

within the stillness,
immense beauty,
peace and tranquility.

left behind—
confusion, desire,
distrust and fear

cast aside—
longing, wishing,
expectation.

embraced—
the moment,
as It is.

serenity develops—
pristine clarity,
as sharp as a knife,
as clear as a bell's ring.

the light of comprehension
banishes all pretence,
mistrust and puzzlement.

no questions, no answers—
just—still.
breathing. simple.

in, out.

• *autobiography*

chilling thoughts

cascading like a veritable Niagara,
the mind's eye disgorges life's
hopes fears and disappointments
as so much litter upon
the debris that is my
conscience and belief.

simultaneously:
joyous, irritated,
resigned, determined,

the unfettered ambition to hold sway
'gainst all prevailing fortune or otherwise,
manifests itself.

gratitude accompanies every waking moment
as the *chemin de fer* partners the rolling stock of travel.

ambition melts into surrender,
disgrace softens its granite face
and unlocks the vault of harmony.

unable to stand aghast,
not finding favour in grief,
tagging along with mirth,
the seasons roll by,
sweetening the flavour
of dusty, empty streets.

immersion in emptiness
is akin to drinking in love's
aftertaste

unable to hold on gracefully,
abandoning all pretence
at understanding and knowledge,

acquisition of which causes only burden
to life's sweet passage,

the silence of joy screams
across the savannah of my imaginings,

murky rainforests of boredom
elbow their way into the frame,
rank smelling, the stench of disheartedness
casting a gloom over proceedings.

always, however,
the resurgence of peace and tranquility
emerging triumphant,
heralding a bright new dawn,
ravaging negativity,
banishing self—
scurrying for cover like so much vermin
the sweet soul music of dissolution and unattachment
to anything in particular.

so be it.

with thanx on my birthday

10th of january

gracious in defeat,
my wondrous
body ~ mind ~ spirit
bows in acquiescence,

and recognises
the most excellent
good fortune
bestowed

of appearance
and awakening in
this place
at this time.

I manifest
eternal homage
and boundless gratitude
to the Shining Light of Existence

for the Treasure
that is my Life.

parenthood

arrgh!

this epithet springs to mind
in contemplating a week
of joy, anger and fun ~
apoplexy with little'n.

yet ~ who grounds me more?
still, who teaches me *[beyond]* my limits?
knowing her, knowing me.

sage of seven years:
wisdom and understanding
beyond the ken of
grumpies like me.

arrgh!

a love totally
without boundaries.

an admiration for
earnest sincerity
of expression
but

[there are no buts . . .]
what you sew you reap
in abundance and,

rewarded and punished beyond measure,
this is the eternal truth of parenthood.

arrgh!

how I give thanks
for the bundle of mirrored frustration
and perpetual beauty ~ clarity
of imagination and refreshment,

always, forgiveness.

aargh!

beatin' the weekend blues

creaking bones,
pain-spangled thighs,
ancient spine,
jangled nerves.

it is but the
jaded mind
that causes
jaded views.

body weary,
mentally upright,
together we can conquer
greater obstacles.

bearing not the weight
of a half-century's toil,

lightly cast aside,
bravely open to elemental realities;
smiling though, joking aside,
ours is a world, a pleasure to ride,

inhaling modesty,
exhaling pride.

~ existing ~

faith in the blossoming of truth;

ahh! the weekend begins!

luxembourg childhood

an aroma of a long departed moment
wafts across my senses,
an indescribable sense of warmth
and well-being suffuses my thoughts.

the taste, the flavour ~
all of a long-gone, cherished, well-worn memory . . .

of times of innocence, times of simplicity,
moments, eternal moments
of unending pleasure and delight
of simple things that presented to my senses.

fear was something never
known in those long-gone days,
awe, wonder and longing for the moment
to last and last.

walking across balmy, windswept grassy fields,
sound of church bells striking sombrely, impassively ~
engendered feelings of indescribable
longing, beauty and aching
in my unformed heart.

never was a moment so clearly,
so bravely etched upon my soul.

to this day, years and years and lifetimes later,
the sound of church bells
echoes the same unwavering melody
of ecstasy and gratitude upon my heart,
within the depths of my Being.

the trip

a moment in time,
as the journey begins.

but this time
there is no return.

thoroughly ill-prepared,
indian sandals, t-shirt, jeans.

a walk across the lakes.
northern england—mountains, streams,
high passes, rocks, wilderness,
alone, but oh so not alone
in nature.

city boy, alone, journeying out
into the unspoiled natural wilderness
of a national park:

awakening, sudden, explosive,
tremendous.
sudden realisation.
this is IT!

so, copious tears
of unbridled love and positive fear,
saltiness streaming down cheeks
as distant shimmering waterfall in yonder vale,

uhhuh,
ohmygod
ohmygoodgod . . .
glory be!

the very first time in ages
(ever?) this being awoke
to a pristine, ageless, beatific,
eternal real world
of shimmering light,
harmony, abundant colour,
smells, space, infinite spaciousness
and companionship from
every blade of grass,
from every speck of dust.

crying, shaking, ecstatic
with joy and fusion with all.

the next hours pass,
burnt forever into eternal memory bank,
thirty-five years since,
(in Dogen's '12 hour time'),
but fused into this moment, that moment,
the forever moment of being time.

crouching down, sandals now melted,
squelching, soaked through
from tracking through fields
of soaking moss and heather.

a stream, a trickle of water
dripping down from one level
of rock to another.

music of the spheres!!

melody! harmony!! the sounds, visceral,
arraigning my senses like nothing on earth,
ludwig's pastorale ~ pedestrian in comparison!
so . . .

thus, resplendent in this earthly paradise,
the young man sits down
like a monarch surveying his kingdom.

a fly, gorgeous, shiny and black as hades,
nestles on the tip of my ear,
sighing, "I love you, I love you"
in my language . . . in our language.

to me, with me, equal to me,
on my level, on our level,
aspects of the same creation,
differentiation dissolved.

oh, and goats and sheep,
the pedestrians of the wild
"hello dude, that's close enough . . ."

eyes casually appraising me,
chewing the cud with rolling jaws
totally unfazed yet
connecting, connected.

now, ascending,
figuratively and metaphorically,
into the realm of sky and space,

monumental realisations bombard
my vision and awareness with increasing intensity;
awe and wonder spill from my limbs and opened mind
like nectar and ambrosia
from the very gates of celestial heaven,

mother nature is in me,
is of me, is me!!

alas! playing 'god'
he sits tremulously
on the steep scree side
of a sheer cliff face,

sitting . . .

then the unexpected yet inevitable moment occurs,
mind leaves body ~ in a flash,

consciousness, eighty metres up in the ether,
hovering, encircling the sitting remains,
seen down below from distant height.

the merest silken thread
connects me to my earthly frame
a league beneath;
excitement fused with terror.

my gaze alters,
seeing the sweep of the round earth
the temptation is to fly, fly away
into the bliss that awaits.

only a frozen moment of indecision
and realisation of the consequences of
this action springs me
back into corporeal frame.

immediately regret is tinged with relief,

"what if ~ what if?"
knowing the choice to be wise—
my time is not yet.

the next period is suffused with biblical images
as previous history is played out on that lonely rock.

wise, now, to the game,
disgorging fabrications at will,
mountains can be erected,
monuments to my all pervasive strength and ego.

ascending toward the peak of lingmell crag,
I turn a corner, a stony path ascends
up, up, up into the clouds,

a long line of people appear,
everyone I have ever known passes by,
as a parade, living and dead,
from myriad prior incarnations,

they are all there, walking, silently.
acknowledgement is there,
but no eye lifts my way
the knowing is there but my invisibility is complete.

the limitless cohort disappears slowly around a narrow ledge,
achingly I tear myself away and gaze fearfully
at the living, cloud-covered peak that is my destiny.

now approaching what must be the zenith,
the path narrows, to either side ~ emptiness,

sheep, looking in amazement,
"what is he doing now? is he out of his mind?"
they transfer their terror into movement
and leap out of my way . . .

now, the Powers, angry,
real mad at my effrontery,
decide to teach me a lesson
I will never forget.

the heavens opened,
a storm of magnificent
and terrible proportion
arose.

alone on a mountain top, barefoot,
(sandals having long ago given up the ghost,)
shredded t-shirt.

icy rain begins to fall, huge slabs of grey rock
like crazy paving are covered in running water,
I slip and slide, out of control.

a cairn of rocks appears out of the mist,
the summit of lingmell crag.
at this very moment, a fork of lightening
flashes in front of my very eyes and is swallowed up by the cairn.

I smell the crackle and hiss and see smoke
curling up above the charred stones, then a crack of thunder
maybe twenty metres or so above me erupts,
splits my terrorized consciousness into a trillion
sharpened shards of annihilation.

never before, or since
have I known such
fear and fright.

yet I came back,
scrambling 'cross near vertical scree
I hurled myself down that mountainside
like a being possessed.

shortly, thankfully
I found myself back in verdant gentle valleys.

far above, the storm argued, ranted and raved,
I cast an occasional glance, fearfully
upward and remembered with trepidation
that moment of crass confrontation
and absurd battle with the mountain gods.

much, much later, curled up in distracted reflection,
a darkened evening spent under the covers
of a warm bed in a hostel for family walkers,

I trembled as I heard the distant thunder
rumbling ominously up on that place where
so long ago, or so it seemed,
I had dared confront the deities
with foolhardy youthful bravado.

I survived,

and held from then on, inordinate respect and
belief in the beauty and strength of natural forces
with which I am, incredibly, inextricably entwined.

of pain accepted, transformed

I am hurting,
nothing hurts as much.

an attack on one's essence
that only flesh and blood can
invoke.

sometimes we have to accept
being the one
to be blamed.

there come times
when we cannot ever
make amends for past history.

for we only see
with one pair of eyes,
one vision, one perspective.

I must accept the pain,
I must bow to the inevitability
that parity, equanimity
and fairness
do not always exist
in the world of
human discourse.

I can be angry,
I can be open to my anger,
I can go to the core ~
and will release the fear, pain
and incomprehension
that travels in my heart
at this awful time.

nether mind

sew tired
knitted brow!
thoughts diffused;
petrified, literally.

sunken, clodden
imprints of the day's activity,
barely recognized.

ideas waft to the surface
to a still small voice,
echoing across
tundra that becomes my mind.

a desolate barren wilderness
of frozen moments.

nether mind!

fuelled by indignation
and puzzlement.

half-formed realisations
are left to fester,
to rot in the pigment of
practical amnesia.

aargh,
nothing that
a coupla lifetimes
sleep won't cure!!

summer's light

all manner of translucent light
trickles, nay—cascades!
through and amongst vibrant
verdant shrubbery at the end of our garden.

little one, loved one, cherished one,
splashes around with gay abandon
in her paddling~pleasure~dome,
as only an 8 year~old~soul can,
drip-feeding our thirsty bay tree
leaning to from an adjacent stone path.

a lightness of feeling pervades the morning air
as I sit here, delivering a discourse of
thanks and gratitude for
this simple pleasure.

twin wonderful souls,
blessed mother and child,
pottering about, filling our lives
with their own summer light.

oh joy!

so tired

so, tired now,
fortitude, stricken down by fatigue,
is running
on empty.

ne'ertheless sweetness prevails,
good heartedness and humility reign,
counter to distressed
inner machinations.

shimmering summer lights
dance across one's gaze,
unconcerned at this observer's mien.

gratefully, gracefully,
life's burden abandoned.

the spring in my step
but a shuffling feat
of imagination.

aroused, I laugh it off:
never gainsay exhaustion—
'tis just another test
upon the merry path
of existence.

sifting

sifting through the
debris of my life,

ever more, uncannily,
pleasant an experience
amongst hastily abandoned projects,
incomplete symphonies.

barriers avoided, terrors left behind,
trails of disquiet disappearing into the distance.

love, dislocated, rampant with
dimly perceived but deeply felt longing.

unmitigated satisfaction and warmth
permeate memories of exploration,
pushing personal boundaries
to their very limits.

arriving at places
that transform and enrich
the myriad possibilities
that exist for those with
vision and courage.

gratitude and completion
spill out like bubbling lava
through leaking pipes,
dissolving mysteriously into the ether,
as ribbons of energy
from the conductor's baton.

time runs out ever rapidly ~
the hourglass feeling disquieteningly
empty and fragile,

yet the moment takes on poignancy;
any traces of bitterness dissolve
in the unfolding awareness
of endings to come.

sifting through the debris of my life,

I thank the Bodhisattvas of consciousness
for welcoming me to this delightful dance and dream,
that continues to advance and impress,
absorb and enrich every breath, every glance.

unmanifest

passed ~ the bewitching hour:
into the awaiting arms of another day.
night clasps my thoughts
in its velvet embrace.

cherished ones, loved ones
cast away in their land of dreams,
only this soul, remote, pondering.

illumination beckons,
yet ultimate intent remains quizzically beyond grasp.
only the inevitability of the untraceable next step leads me on.

*(if I had known then what I now know
all would have been so different)*

merely to recognize the imperturbable nature of fate is to enlighten,
'tis incumbent to unfold the burden of guilt and self-recrimination
that, from time to time, casts such a
stranglehold on my spirit.

it is now time to relinquish all thought
and rest peacefully,
trusting in the natural grace of the Eternal to propel
me towards the light that silently awaits
at the close of this infinite darkness.

a mantra for today

now ~ a clearer world,
a fresh approach;
sunlight has never
shone like this before,

out of the ashes
of yesterday's pain,
emergent joy,
triumphant again.

forgiveness is a blessing;
doth warrant bestowal
upon our tenuous
sense of self.

time and again
and time and again,
relinquishing fears,
absorbing pain.

these sentiments
never loosen their hold
'pon translucent frame.

now ~ a clear world,
a fresh approach.
sunlight has never
shone like this before,

out of the ashes
of yesterday's pain,
emergent courage,
triumphant again.

wretched

raging torrents of emotion
spill forth, clawing, spewing;
enormous breath of bile and brood,
wanting to get on with it.

dying to 'hit the mark,' ~
falling short, purpled angst
parades scorn 'cross fevered brow.

haunting echoes of derision,
a distant threat of disapproval ~
mocking, to die for, to kill for,
turning away from reason.

the deliberation of hatred ~
thus far travelled,
nothing begun, nowhere reached,

the wretched insanity of falling prey
to the transparency of anger.

holidays

holidays
are like
holy days.

without agenda,
save to
relish, savour
and apprehend
the simpler aspects
of living.

reminding
oneself to
let go of worldly concerns,
aspirations and goals.

learning to be present,
fully, wholly,
without the slightest rancour,
longing or movement
away from the here and now.

ahh! simple
pleasures,
sweet simplicity!
holidays
are holy days
indeed.

oops!

bumping up to the edges of things,
it just does not quite add up.
I was robbed today ~
I bow deeply to the misfortune,

and I thank the whirling mysterious merry go round of life
for graciously reminding me of my ephemerality
and for the peripheral nature of my existence
alongside the grand scheme of things.

today did not quite make the grade,
but ne'ertheless was quite beautiful
in an unanswerable and inexplicable way.
I dropped things, I missed things ~

just didn't quite 'get it',
I served, I sat, gave thanks,
messed up ~ all grist to the mill;
tomorrow is another day.

I pray for the chance
to move alongside the mayhem
and cruise happily, mindful of my little self
learning his place in a big wide world
that whirls forth indiscriminately, thirsting only for
channels of growth and productivity ~ regardless.

praise be
little me, praise be!!

she

this rolling earth, warm umbilica
drawing breath, encrusted,
pasted 'pon my heart,
desires, running deep.

fiery subterranean furnace,
kindling, fuelling rawness in my soul
drawn unerringly, irresistibly
closer, closer to extinction.

I want to lose myself in this
I want to lose myself, oh the taste, the texture ~
manna to my tortured senses,
heavenly mirage forever beyond grasp.

the paradox of it is in the bleakness
of consummation ~ the truth is shallow, ephemeral
the greater the urgency, the more desperate the plight,
the sheer folly—the sheer delight.

banished by reason, slighted by sanity,
ignored by knowledge, this fateful embrace,
this massive disgrace, my shadow atremble
'pon fear of discovery.

this yearning, this turning,
this pitching, this burning,
alight, alight from my fractured vessel
and give me peace—give me space
to dissolve your embrace,
your power and omnipotence.

farewell mother, farewell.

wishing well

less desirous, less expectant,
clearer does my life become.

the nearer approaching
an unabashed openness and humility,
the richer does my experience manifest
simplicity, goodness and transparency.

so very hard to relinquish cherished habit;
the key to wisdom is to see one's attachment
just for what it is.

a barrier to development,
mara holding one back
to control, dominate
ultimately to deaden,
defuse joy and abandon.

never will I encourage a grasping mind,
forever vigilant 'gainst the temptation
to possess.

I want an open heart,
I wish for nothing more.

gladly do I disinherit all worldly aspiration,
just to dwell in the heart
of the moment.

forsake all inheritance
save a full life lived
with honesty and
integrity.

a ramble

such gentle amble
through an afternoon's
retreat ~no goal,
no scurry, time to look around.

a placid landscape echoes the sweep
through personal history
that runs parallel
to my itinerary.

so much to ponder
so many moments
to savour, regret
and wonder.

all these events
leaning, simply,
to now.

from whence they flow,
many tributaries ~
chance, destiny
call it what you will:

knowledge, deep in one's heart,
that it all makes 'perfect sense,'
yet in truth lies far
beyond rational grasp.

moments stolen from the copybook
of circumstance.

such gentle amble
through an afternoon's
retreat ~no goal,
no scurry, time to look around.

my vow

it is not enough to speak and write well,
nor enough to be seen to be
doing the right thing.

it is only enough
when life IS justly discharged
in the light and action of truth.

when nobody sees, and no one knows—
a cloak of invisibility obscures rightful deeds
performed in the right way
simply because: that IS the way to be.

I vow, therefore,
never to write another word
which seeks to redeem me
without aspiration to live a nobler life.

too often the word is disaffected in the deed,
vouchsafe, not another phrase will escape my pen,
save to countenance a thought
that is practiced in endeavour
and realized in accomplishment.

these are the best of times

when breath courses through
unwitting frame,
doth joy spring up
'midst sentient pain.

glory of glories!
alive, to feel the breath
of humanity—
in all its illogic.

no rhyme, no reason,
the history of relationship
steers crazily to and fro.

erratic course,
subject to neither system nor lore,
save whim and caprice
of dullened mind.

how I love to hate the jalousie!
how I steer wide berth to
those whose fortune hinders mine.

like senseless animal,
careening wildly,
out of touch with
hear~say or there~say.

mindless to the call of whit,
enquiry or destiny,
I blather wildly,
delivering no real substance.

how I cackle and haw,
meander and prevaricate,
stiffened and wizened,
ignoring the call of the sane.

when breath courses through
unwitting frame,
doth joy spring up
'midst sentient pain.

gladly let it be,
and ring the hollow laugh
of the disenfranchised citizen.
these are the best of times.

- *nature*

eternal globe of light

I sit back
contentedly.

ahh! blessed touch,
softly, sweetly
caressing my shoulders—
that unsurpassable glow,

thou wondrous globe!

radiating 'cross
ninety three million leagues:
vacant love,
azure light,

silently, speedily arriving,
whispering molecules
of pure energy
into the parchment
of my soul,

life freely given,
freely shared
with one and all,

sun, of god.

fête~full ode

oh! flippant
august rain,
falling
again, again
and again.

palms plaintively
pressed
'gainst windowpane.

oh! fickle sunlight,
show thy face,
rekindle the joy
that is thy grace!

summer too soon
its death rattles sound,
autumn crooks it's
fateful finger,

despondencies abound.

dawning

blessed nectarine globe,
appearing gently 'pon
distant horizon.

unfailing deliverance,
dispelling demons
of nocturnal disquiet.

fathomless embryo,
spreading warmth,
enlightening, awakening,
attending to nature's call
of fecundity.

from beginningless time
humankind has turned
its face upward,
trusting your eternal flame,

unremitting faith in your endless
bestowal of life and light,

we live by you.

Ss ~ now

ahhh.
the crispness!

horizontal flurries,
a zillion unique shapes
float crazily by,
twisting and turning,
this way and that.

but in that
soft, soft silence
that is so special
to bitter cold days.

how I adore
the quiescence of
the coldest winter's eve,

that special light—
reflected white,
somnambulant awareness,
sweet sweet melancholy,
one step removed from
remorse.

yet the merest thread
of life bringing with it
tumultuous
emotion and joy.

sceane

in praise of the dorset coastline #1

south coast ~ mellow sea
hugging up to soft chalk,
caressing the boundaries of the land
slowly, minutely eroding the territory,
nibbling away like so many mice,
reminding the dissipating land mass
of its ephemerality.

what a delightful marriage of sea and sky!
soft greyness merging,
melting away into one another
as supreme lovers do.

an understated undulation,
the rolling tide shapes the shore,
designs the glory
of the lands contour.

the soft, soft whisper of salty spray,
coaxing its way deftly, smoothly,
tantalizingly, through alleyways
of a zillion trillion pebbles,

shaped in endless circles
by the unflappable, unstoppable
moon-crazed waters
of the ocean floor.

I feel at home ~ here,
a part of things.
I wish to stay and drink in
the perfumed ambrosia of nature
on her own terms.

I will return.

ineffable

in praise of the dorset coastline #2

knee~deep in movement,
thoughts bestride me: consecration.

yonder, bonny wild horses gently graze,
their luxuriant brown coats glide
softly, serenely 'gainst
prickly, sharp yellow gorse.

the contrast pleases me,
sweet salty air penetrates
my inner meanderings,
I cast a gladdened eye around:

all is perfect just as it is,
a moment that remains eternal.

I tramp this way and that, foiling distraction,
willing only to savour this moment as it is.

eventually I reach the waters edge,
gulls sit astride barren rocks
impassive, majestic.

querulous currents argue the toss amongst each other
and disgorge the remnants of their ideas
carelessly onto the rocky outcrop
that has become my temporary abode.

carefree and satiated,
I open my arms and my mind
unto the panorama that encircles me,

breathing in deeply ~
It is I ~ I am It
oh glory be,
glory be!

sitting in the rain

plip plop
plipp loplip
plopplip plopplip
pluush.

persistent
precipitation
pervades my privacy!

and yet,
opening to its
temperate rhythm
becomes a teaching.

intimate,
familiar and
the very sound of life.

how I love
nature's cleansing,
drops
coursing down the windowpane!

only *we* interpret such
action as melancholic.

such character and disposition
of pre-prandial dialogue
enriches the soil
and informs
the soul.

song for africa

how I love Africa,
land of beauty, rising star
how I long for Africa,
miss my fam'ly from afar.

walking thru' the mango groves,
watching mothers washing clothes,
joy and light burst in my heart,
from where, I'm sure they'll never part.

how I love Africa,
land of beauty, rising star
how I long for Africa,
miss my fam'ly from afar.

strolling by a gentle sea,
water lapping at my feet,
white sand, ahh! as warm as toast,
beautiful Swahili coast.

how I love Africa,
land of beauty, rising star
how I long for Africa,
miss my fam'ly from afar.

Amboseli paradise,
I rose at dawn to see the sights,
wildlife grazing freely there,
all I did was stand and stare.

how I love Africa,
land of beauty, rising star
how I long for Africa,
miss my fam'ly from afar.

"jambo Kenya, how are you"?
Love you madly, never blue,
"abari Kenya, see you soon!"
you're in my heart, forever true.

how I love Africa,
land of beauty, rising star
how I long for Africa
miss my fam'ly from afar.

taking stock

clarity and light being my watchwords
of our glorious 'indian summer'.

how I love this time of year ~
late september,
that timeless moment
'twixt summer and fall.

sharpness in the air,
crystalline transparency,
a delicate dance of hope,
expectancy and fulfillment.

the melancholy of fall, the slipping away
of yet another fertile chapter
in one's earthy tirade,
is around the corner, seen dimly at dawn.

the delight and ecstasy of summer
a still memorable reality,
discovery of new worlds, tastes, sights
and sounds engorging the palette.

a moment to take stock,
breathe in deeply, savour the moment,
the joyous light dancing and spinning
around verdant corridors of perception.

a chance to give thanks
for the prestige and privilege
of inhabiting this human form.

an opportunity to pledge,
with fullness of heart,
to live this sanctified existence
to the very utmost of our abilities.

with bows.

wind

wind
sending leaves
crackling 'cross the sidewalk,
winter symphony.

surf breathing

it struck me this morning whilst sitting,
the amazing correspondence between breathing
and the rhythm of the surf
at ocean's edge.

indescribable thrill of natural breath
working autonomously,
day in day out,
on and on.

deep satisfaction of the
effortless drawing in of oxygen,
then exhalation of used air,
gently dispelled from frame,
again and again
and again.

how marvelous would it be
if the rhythm of one's breath
was as tranquil as the
ineffable meandering of surf!

imagine if you will breathing in as the pull of
thousands of kilometres of water
drags salty foam across the sand.

many moments later,
fresh ripples of foam cascade mightily forward,
breaking laterally along
beach's infinite width.

another moment, another breath,
eternal repose.

zenith

as the year reaches it summer climax,
our oval globe turns its northern face
inexorably closer toward the sun,
giver of beam and glow.

the verdant vegetation swells,
surrendering in humid intensity.
the very soil purrs in fecundity,
its serpentine inhabitants
wriggling this way and that,
providing the ether that fertilizes
and gives succour to all manner of life.

I too behold a passion, an excitement
that swells within my breast, filling
me with hope and elation.

I arise early ~ already the sky, grey green,
presages the brilliant dawn that
comes apace and unchallenged.

a buoyant optimism abounds,
still on the right side of time,
the days gathering length and pace,
always the promise of longer days to come.

fuelling, like the most marvelous orchestra
of myriad perceptions, a gathering
crescendo of happiness and light.

noisily chattering, the sky~life flitters
this way and that, bound for nowhere—
existing merely in this very
moment, for its own sake.

seemingly far distant, that uncalled for zenith ~
the peak, the turning point,
subliminally obscured and presently redundant.

the moment when all manner of truths alight,
and an autumnal murmur gathers pace,
silently seeking its role in our unforeseen advance
into a new age.

but, for the moment let us savour this freshness
and give thanks for this annual pilgrimage
toward the golden light.

a delightful amble

suffolk countryside—emergent with calm:
we strode out on a mid—november morning,
gentle earth surrendering to our tread.

pacific sunbeams, tawny yellow, reflecting the late season,
sparkling 'cross fecund softly rolling fields.

shafts of ochre brilliance reflecting through
bright—green blades of grass,
creating a kaleidoscopic dazzle.

the lonesome craw of crow, a scampering rabbit—
a late season swallow flickering through broken bough.

reflective banter and enquiry flowing effortlessly 'twixt us,
two long—time, loving, life—long voyagers.

at each turn, nature's delight and surprise:
a stately fox, big amongst deep brown rolling turf,
playful amongst scavenger birds, tail held proudly aloft,
free from human interference and burden.

here and there, shards of flint,
propped up in sticky brown sod,
crystalline, reflecting autumnal loam.

at last, the vista opens,
eyes raised to behold a panorama of emollient serenity,
scattered trees, fields, shimmering gaily in a light blue haze
far as the eye can see, quietly rolling on, acre 'pon acre,
mile upon mile, into the far distant expectation
of that which lies beyond.

we pause to take stock—an infinite peace reigns,
a memory, unspoken but deeply felt,
of the timeless expanse of earth's story
susurrates and unfolds.

we ramble on, past gaily painted farmsteads
with their ancient east—anglian eaves
pointing sharply toward the starched, azure heavens.

we arrive presently amongst local cottages
a return to habitation—and habituation.

a magnificent pastoral church,
flag of the union flapping sombrely in the autumnal haze
from its imposing dark age, square turreted tower,
holds centre stage 'midst country commune.

'in our thoughts . . .'

silently, entering through a beamed corridor,
breathing deeply the ancient woody, ethereal odour of medieval worship,
I gaze up admiringly at latticed wood beams
which protect and sustain the longevity
of faith and submission.

I stand, muted for a moment, taking in the tranquility,
remembrance of young lives, lost.
so I may now stand here in stillness and glory,
humbled and grateful, awed and a' fear
of those withering young souls' dreadful plight,
precious wreaths gathered 'gainst whitewashed,
pinched walls and galleries of wooden benches
like so many numbed soldiers holding forth.

I give thanks and finish our delicious
affray into this timeless landscape
by building a hearty, crackling wood fire
in our hidden, crumbling hideaway
deep in this memorable suffolk paradise,
reflecting on the glory and wonderment
of unspoiled natural harmonies we beheld.

- *to loved ones/friends*

for Alexis

blessed am I
with wondrous child,
the gods upon my fate
have smiled!

awaiting in the wings
some purpose as yet undefined,
shallow movements
belie subtle depths.

so, full of thought as she is,
has my best interests at heart,
oft while I gaze anxiously her way,
a vague, undefined angst
flirts across my brow,

I wonder what life has
for her; as history unfolds:
dear lord be kind!

I adore from both near
and from afar,
both caring and
cared for.

for our love is pure,
unsullied and joyful;
it matters not the huge divide,
our paths forever coincide.

just like the earth

just like the earth
beneath your feet
I am not merely
fair weather friend.

whatever your step
light, joyful and carefree,
or downtrodden, morose,
cornered and dark,

just like the earth,
will I be there to hold you
in gentle embrace—

to add spring to
your moments of joy,
and a place to rest your weary body,
at times of vulnerability
and need for succour,

just like the earth.

just when

light headed ~ conscience clear,
littl'n sad, no puddin' ~ oh dear!

should I rush to the shop
and appease her gloom?
or let things be,
(she should not assume.)

my humour goes down unsung,
no clowning can get by her resolve,

please her ~ or doom!

~ to Terrie ~

my love

words, being vehicles,
are not strong enough to convey
the love, gratitude and infinite grace
that engulf me upon the most fortuitous unraveling
of my journey on this planet.

especially, most especially
for the unadorned great fortune at
having by my side a beautiful woman,
a tender and upright soul, one who
allows me my thoroughly self-centred conduct.

someone who came to me at the very moment
that my fortunes changed, to accompany me
upon the latter stages of my present journey,
showing me unrestricted love, enabling me
to resurrect my self-belief and to turn around the spiral
of chagrin into which I had sunk.

thinking about the circumstances of our fortuitous meeting,
it surely came as no surprise—
for at an early age, perhaps around five or six,
I use to dream of her, my perfect, loving and beautiful soul mate.
we were to do everything together, and as one
the boundless joy and happiness we found in each other's company
would form an armour of unimpeachable happiness
into which none of the world's bitter misfortunes could penetrate.

I knew in my heart that this was no mere dream,
but a talisman of immense precipitation.

the following forty years were not happy ones—
a broken home, then being cast away into a cold emotionally sterile
world led to a young life of dissolution and reckless self absorption.

yet the dream quietly smouldered away in the background,
fuelling me through hard times, lonely times,
melancholy times and blue times.

then, half a lifetime later, one quiet, unprepossessing saturday,
she walked into my life—I did not recognize her at first,
when light enters, a blind person merely perceives
a subtle change of atmosphere, but does not behold the brilliance.

miracle of miracles, the hand of kismet restored my vision,
allowing me redress and my aging but ageless dream
cast off its slumber and became reality.

now, many years later, the incredible weight of time
presses against my mortal frame and,
in perceiving the final turn of events,
causes me both joy and sorrow alike.

to be apart from her is something unimaginable,
yet this certainty grows daily stronger.
I only hope, at my passing, our shared time will have cast
a loving radiance across her path and
allow her solace upon her remaining travels.

our love will definitely live on through the wondrous fruits of
our union—a bright loving daughter who will
carry our love into the uncharted reaches of the future.

god bless you my intrepid young
family for my greatest
good fortune.

~ to Al ~

like a brother

from way back when, lost in the haze of time,
but firmly etched in the bosom of my fondest memories,

there you stand, tall and strong, my role model,
my early hero, master of such triumphs
as chess, mastering ancient Hebrew and—later on,
super-cool teenager with trendy clothes and stylish sideburns.

many adventures did we share hitching 'cross sunburst France
in the mid sixties, endless supply of amazing
anecdotes, funny, scary and joyous.

perhaps a seminal moment: sleeping under the luminescent sky and shooting
stars in the corn-fields of Cambrai, the youthful passion of freedom, wonder
and excitement eternally burned into the most treasured archive of my
personal history.

sharing an impossibly tiny Fiat with an enormously smelly Italian,
sharing a smooth, iconic American automobile with a pretentious Swiss pop star
a coffee machine by his gear stick and a 'personal frennd of ze rolling stones.'

sharing the autobahn with a paranoid German who ditched us
in the mittel of no-vair as "ve ver going to kill him!"
and of course being kidnapped in Schweitzer by a coupla gay Italian Mafioso
and taken not to our chosen destination, France, but the
highways and byways of north Italia.

(hugging floor in Nice airport in sleeping bags.)

they go on and on, these wonderful carefree times,
sauntering merrily along with love and affection for
one another, which none could break apart.
later we lose touch, but not mutual warmth and affection.

and now, God knows in the twilight years
scarce possible to imagine WE would GROW OLD!
dearest cuz, I love you dearly and you
will always be in the front row of my life-dreams.
enjoy your day—celebrate with pride sixty hard won years
and raise a glass to our loving well-spent youth together.

in praise of a true Bodhisattva—Jesus Christ

how I truly love this Holy person,
one who brought humanity back to mankind
with sensitivity, intelligence and humility.

regardless of the pressures of reported history one way or t'other,
it is impossible for a reasoned thinker not to be awed
by this Man's impeccability and integrity.

I refuse to be swayed, by virtue of my received birth—Semitic,
nor by impassioned advocates of doctrine
who would endeavour to force me into an either/or stance
that would led me only into fear of adopting a untenable position
that casts me into the fires of hell.

I know only that He led an entirely blameless existence;
no stain of evil crossed his actions—ever,
despite immense and sustained provocation.

what an example for us all!
His life was, is and will always be a joy to behold.
He has brought me immense faith in the finest,
absolute potential of human enterprise.

as only a handful of people in humanity's shared, short history
I respect him inordinately, and am immeasurably grateful
to know his works and wondrous explanations,
thoughts, perspectives and championing of the underprivileged.

if only we could, as a complete and seamless world,
accept his teachings without division and judgment,
would we find commensurate peace, joy
and fulfillment in our lives.

golden peaches

bless!
Zappa lives on,
through the excitement
and appreciation of a modern day
nine and three-quarter year old lass,

the delights of discovering creativity and humour
and true excellence of melody
has enriched her experience.

to pass on these musical nuggets
is a joyful and important
task for us 'grumpies,'

as Uncle Frank said,
(via Varese:)

*'the present day composer
refuses to die!'*

for Nico ~ 'wacha kelele wewe pumbafu!'

friendship

dear old friend!
parallel journeys ~ worlds apart,
yet underlying bonds of mutual respect and love.

both of us reaching that mirage
of maturity and wisdom from
life's experience.

so many fine memories of our shared schooldays,
we were a counterbalance to each other:
you ~ steady, sober, focused,
me ~ wild, erratic, a dreamer.

however, this delicate balance
of opposites underpinned a fine friendship
and a lifelong mutual admiration.

how you regaled me with amazing stories
of your adventures and exploits of your East African childhood,
belying your steady mien,
you lived dangerously in those early days.

how you were there for me, with wisdom and foresight,
tho' unable to prevent me from self-destruction.

yet you never judged, but kept your
side of the bargain, listened gravely to my
stories of madness and woe.

I look forward to continuing our association
into the mists of eternal old age,
safe in the knowledge that
we will forever hold each other
dearly in our hearts.

- *potpourri*

without redemption

with fractured smile and numbed thought,
a vast array of images scud across my brow
in celluloid procession.

a breeze blows steadily through
dappled green poplars, which line the empty avenues,
distant church bells toll mournfully
across a windswept plain.

a lone figure, black in relief,
clutching a sodden scarlet cloth,
creeps silently 'cross fields of heather,

awestruck, crying copious tears of gratitude,
unaware of silent eyes watching,
takes a swift turn into cobbled streets,
glistening with early morning rain.

a distant scream, shuffling feet,
the drag of legs across a gritted pavement;
behind the blackened door,
she has breathed her last.

with crazy grin, our lonely figure
disappears in an instant, clutching a
lifetime of bitter memories,
brittle bones in a gnarled ugly fist.

'goodnight my love ~ farewell'
for the flight from this temporal dream finally begins,
for you no shaft of redeeming light,
no empty corridor to blessed release,

save an eternal reaching out for light and warmth
that never materializes and remains forever
beyond your grasp.

dreamed

struggling blindly with his burden,
the afflicted man persevered along the barren road.

the way was long, the climate severe.
distant memories of sunnier climes
flashed across his thoughts
tempering his imagination and fuelling his despair.

he dreamed of homecoming,
yet no home was his to bear.
he dreamed of tender arms
willing him to embrace,

but such comfort was only a bitter
canvas long ago shredded into
the cracks of his lonely travail.

turning his gaze heavenward, eyes fluttering
in desperate search, willing himself to conjure up
a beneficent presence, everlastingly
to sooth his fevered frame.

none was forthcoming, and he settled himself,
forward, to pursue a lonely, endless trek
upon a desolate, unforgiving tundra.

and yet, unbeknownst to him
at this time, fortune was to play out
a gentler cadence, to alter
once and for all his twisted drama.

far ahead on distant shore,
a merest thought, a deific wave
of generosity and forgiveness
lay in wait, patiently, fortuitously,

planning to overturn this wretched person's fortune.
'hail fellow traveler, on life's misfortunes well drank deep!'

the inaudible cry of his conscience
reverberated silently across the eternal emptiness,
the entire cosmos reduced to the
plaintive cry of a tortured soul.

upon what, in all this boundless universe
could our poor wretch console himself?

a light, feeble at first,
flickering, darting this way and that,
served to distract his worst imaginings.

then, fleetingly yet unerringly,
the great unanswered torment began miraculously to repeal.

our pathetic hero threw himself down and begged revelation,
uttering senseless yet deeply felt
 prayer to
a deity, as yet unknown, as yet unborn,
imagined beyond wildest dreams.

a hand, outstretched, warmth personified,
clasped his shaking frame,
drew him near and uttered those gifted phrases
of forgiveness, welcome and encouragement.

for sanity had returned and distant horrors
became the receding nightmare
of false habit and exclusivity.
'welcome man, welcome to the human domain.'

the 'blues'

frettin', slidin', screamin', crying,

achin', bakin' ~ meooh!~ zik making.

liein', sighing, singin', flying,

kickin', purring, prayin', dieing,

sole food—settin' the mood

I lurve the bloos!!

manual of digital dexterity

hands ~ crab-like embracing keyboard,
friendly creatures at callers behest,
wondrous servants ~ hands,
a lifetime spent refining, learning caressing.

many kinds of action, always serving, never disobedient:

seeking companionship, never happier than when held together,
cosmic mudra, fingertip to fingertip,
rounded flesh, at base of thumb, chicken-like drumstick
nestling contentedly against symmetrical rival.

that is the point, working in tandem,
helping each other out ~ no rivalry,
working together to get the job done.

politicians would profit from studying
these wonders of compromise,
each accepting the role of the other,
stronger hand nestling beneath weaker:

protective, maternal ~ weaker member,
always on hand to provide cover, support,

never happier than when,
fingers pointing upward at the heavens
thanks given for a miracle
of skeletal engineering,

no wonder the digital age has come!
ready to shake, affording a cheery wave;
thumbs up, to the practical creator
of our ten piece wonder-manuals,

handzzz!!

morsels

joy is in awakening to an inexplicable clarity,
joy is in the earnest expression on your child's face.
joy is never expected!
joy is in noticing a glance from a loved one that is only for you.

love is in warmth.
love is in wishing the best for all sentient beings,
love is in putting others before yourself.
love is in a smile of recognition, passing by a stranger ~
love **is**.

happiness is in allowing things to be just as they are.
happiness is in seeing the beauty of your surroundings,
happiness is in fulfillment without any expectation.

fear is in the absence of joy, love and happiness.
fear is founded on attachment, ignorance and craving.

greed is in allowing the 'little self' to call the shots.
greed is subtle, insidious and dangerous.
greed needs to be rooted out.

delusion is in believing you are real.
delusion is in hoping against hope that things will work themselves out
for your benefit only.
delusion is dissipated by recognizing the limitations of
intellectual and visceral craving.

joy, love and happiness,
fear, greed and delusion ~ which drive you?
food for reflection ~
ideas for being in a bigger, brighter space.

unremitting longing ~ *reflections on the plight of Tibetans*

as a living, breathing,
vibrantly conscious being,
it hurts me so.

in my heart
a wretched sadness reigns.

unanswerable questions
scream their daily message into
the very fabric of my being,

why oh why does this earthly colossus
feel so threatened, so insecure
as to disallow these glorious people
the inalienable right to live lives of their own choosing?

and at their spiritual head, His Holiness,
a true, real, living example
of righteousness, integrity, infinite patience
and good will personified.

I too have a dream ~ one day
freedom and joy will be the birthright
of all beings.

no fear, no insecurity,
just acceptance of difference
and celebration of variety.

until then, in my heart
a wretched sadness reigns.

yes

we make the judgment,

meanwhile the earth spins,

mind moves,

mud slides.

guy dense from you-TH!

if I take the time,
words emerge ~ sublime.

when I think apace,
manifesting faith.

not shrinking from truth,
living on the hoof.

strange as it seems,
love spills forth ~ in reams.

aching to perform, making the grade,
displaying 'certitude',
declaring "fit for purpose."
these things are basically sound.
seldom found, gone to ground.

nothing ever out of place.
seldom losing face.
no need to make haste,
belief in oneself ~ finding the ace,

in your life ~ forever,
spliced with vigour,
attitude and grace.

'old blighty'
on returning to UK after holiday in europe

greeting the returning albion,
'old blighty'
puts on a brave face.

grudgingly forgiving one
the insouciance of betrayal.

mainland europe has many attractions ~
great food, marvelous architecture,
stunning scenery,

but after awhile, 'old blighty' beckons
with her scruffy apparel, dire humour,
open arms to all comers with a sense of
fair play and decency,

but best of all,
a real non-judgmental
and laissez faire approach to life;

gawd bless
you mam.

brrrr!

we all try

notwithstanding desolation, incomprehension and despair
I see daily, myriad manifestations of divine glory
in our efforts to 'make a fist' of our lives.

I cannot but reflect curiously on human nature
and our propensity to abide in melancholy.

whence our need for comfort, appreciation
and recognition?

have we fallen so far from God's grace,
love and warmth?

"abide in Me"
saith the Lord,
(with tranquility.)

we need continuous pampering, cosseting,
so lost, so needy,
so dependent on social praise.

I know this in myself ~
I see this in others.

hence constantly am enamoured
of the smile, nod, wink and
tender touch of encouragement.

oh to inhabit a world where all feel valued,
equal under the sun and the society
of humankind!

reed allowed!

fluffy, airy puffs of moisture,
tingling—trickle down
from vaporized ether.

dance of fruition,
the breath of knowing—
a grasp of the unfeigned,
a gasp of the surreal.

fragmentary forgetfulness,
our earth turns.
some universal smiling,
an unknowing wink.

all is well,
embraceable you,
embraceable us,
it had to be ~ thus.

abundant affirmation:
spin a thought
for your dissolution

a grasp of the authentic,
a gasp of the surreal.

all is well,
embraceable you,
embraceable us,
it will be ~ thus.

PART II

~ Prose ~

- *travelogues*

les trois soeurs

(Having most recently returned from a fun-filled, sun-kissed fortnight in one of the most beautiful environs on the planet, I am back to share with you my beatitudes)

oh provence, blessed mediterranean paradise where cicadas blow your mind with sound and sun blows your soul with light and energy.

'les trois soeurs'—these are the 3 sister cistercian 12th century abbeys in provence: having spent two days meditating in and sketching two of these wondrous buildings: silvacane abbey and senanque abbey, I can share with you their simple and profound beauty and silence. (the third—le thoronet, reputedly the most beautiful of the three I will have to wait to see—it was beyond my reach this time.)

850 years of silence and contemplation resound winningly through my soul: I wandered around and around in complete and utter ecstasy for hours on end, touching the beautifully crafted stone arches and walls, breathing in the surreal smells of dust and depth, gasping with awe in the marvelously sculptured spaces where even my insubstantial voice echoed sweetly in simple harmonies and melody.

I sat spellbound in silence and lost myself in untrammeled simplicity and Moment in darkened corners lit up by beams of glorious sunlight.

I sat in baking sun and drew with all the love and skill I could muster the simple and time-honoured form of great architecture and design.

no grandiose affectation here in these honest lines—the shape, form and structure of these imperial buildings will last an eternity and outlive all manner of fashion and ephemeral pretence.

the simplicity and reality of simple arches, symmetry—light and darkness, simply shook my sensibilities to the core and I will carry their beauty, reality and perfection with me eternally wherever I breathe.

provenance

This true story was inspired by 8-year-old daughter asking me to tell her about my life:

The time: fall, 1969-70

The place: Northern Europe/Scandinavia

I left school in summer '69; in fact, the day after I left, Neil Armstrong set foot upon the moon: how auspicious was that! I had spent 10 years 'locked away' in a boarding school, having watched the Sixties float merrily by. I had waited patiently, studying hard, achieving university status a year early—thus had a 'gap' year before that was invented, to live it up, hence was really looking forward to tasting, more savouring the outside world all to myself.

Innocent 17 years, ready to dive headfirst into the hedonism and naive spirituality that was the times. I had prepared—my closest companion those last seven years had been my guitar which I had lived with as closely guarded lover through teenage ups and downs: no mean blues player, I could jam it up with the best of 'em.

So, having spent the autumn as a hostel worker in trendy downtown Kensington, London and acquiring an address book full of Scandinavian beauties, I packed up my rucksack and guitar and headed off down the A2 to Dover, ready to taste the fruits of freedom and hitch-hike around Northern Europe with the abandon and carefree spirit of youth unattached (these were the days of 'free love'.)

Fast forward to: spring '70. I awoke one morning, staying by a frozen lake close to the town of Rovaniemi on the Arctic circle—Lapland/Finland, having spent 6 amazing months travelling the frozen North (images of hearing Coltrane for the first time on headphones in the local public library, his mellifluous cadences and spirituality unfreezing my juvenile mind and opening it up to the beauty of free music)—I was TIRED of snow—having literally not seen a flower or greenery for over 6 months, I decided there and then—the Mediterranean, the South was where I had to be.

Fast forward to: March 21st 1970.

Having hitched/walked my way down non-stop from the Gulf of Bothnia in Finland to Gothenburg, Southern Sweden, a distance of about 1300 kilometres, I was in pretty bad shape: virtually penniless, hungry as hell (had not eaten cooked food since leaving Rovaniemi some 4 days hence) and cold, cold as ice; I had walked through 2 nights of blizzard without catching a ride, had struggled knee-deep in snow through sodden, dark pine forests.
I finally reached the Gothenburg—Fredrikshavn (Denmark) ferry terminal, completely exhausted from travel, cold and hunger. I got out my trusted guitar and sat down outside the terminal and strode out some Robert Johnson bottleneck blues until I had made enough Kroner to buy a ticket across the straits to Denmark.

Tramping onto the ferry, I had my first glimpse of 'civilization' since setting off from my friend Kaarina's home by a frozen lake in Lapland: light, warmth and the unbelievable smell of cooked food.

I ignored in a well-rehearsed and practiced way the disdainful looks and sneers of the local travelers and found my way to the cafeteria and checked out the menu: meatballs and potatoes, AWESOME!! : 12 Kroner . . . I checked in my bedraggled coat pockets—one Kroner, one measly Kroner to my name!

Well, I could at least get a coffee, better than nothing, I figured; on my way round to the bar, I caught sight of a couple of one-armed bandits. With nothing to lose (well, everything, actually, but as it was fortune favoured the bold), I stuck my last money in the world into this mechanical trickster and pulled the handle. For what seemed like an eternity, the three balls whizzed around noisily, I can remember it so clearly AND stopped. With a curious vomiting sound, this blessed machine spat out 12 Beautiful Kroner!!!

I looked up—'there IS a God', I thought, I can't tell you the emotion I experienced at that moment, but it was heaven-sent.

Needless to say, I went round and bought my favourite meatballs and potatoes; I will leave to your imagination as to how they tasted . . .

Many more adventures befell me in that magical year 'off the rails.'

Kilimanjaro—the biggest mountain I've never seen

Kenya Notebook

(text and 5 poems)

Friday 25th July 2008—2:45pm ~ Flight.

I start writing this log 37K feet above Libya, over the Sahara Desert—as I look out of the plane and downward, all I can see is orange—sand covers the earth as far as the eye can see in all directions; since we passed the North African coast flying south, parched, scorched earth has dominated the landscape, hour after hour.

Awesome journey. After leaving Heathrow—10 minutes to the coast, bouffant clouds across the channel, into patchwork fields of Northern France. Very soon, the Rhone valley, a deep scar running down the east side of France; we banked east—the Alps appear, majestically covered in snow. Before too long, we hit the Cote d'Azure and the Mediterranean flashes—shimmering by. Caught Corsica, Sardinia, flew over the west side of Sicily and soon spotted Malta, like a jewel in the iridescent blue sea—a tiny, tiny island, the whole thing clear as a bell. Another stage across the southern Med and then . . . . Libyan coast spread out staggeringly in both directions—Africa—no sign of life, any roads, and habitation—NOTHING, except sand.

Halfway there now—am in unexplored territory and heading further south than I have ever been; excitement mounts. As the time rolls by, names appear on the flight screen—Darfur (terror, war, famine), Khartoum, Addis Ababa (romance, intrigue, history), meanwhile the view is always the same, sand, hour after hour. The globe turns and the sun's glare softens, cumulus clouds appear beneath like so much cotton wool—empty, peaceful and desolate, southern Sudan.

Sunset is absolutely glorious! Recently flew through a storm—littl'un (Alexis) grew scared, massive clouds banked, stretching up to way over 50K feet—lightening flashes, turbulence; we are now reaching equatorial country, softer, greener, mountainous, what a wonderful view of our lovely planet.

Saturday 26th July 2008

We arrived in Nairobi at 9:15pm last night—talk about an African welcome, queued for 2 hours to get our visas, only to discover that half of our luggage had been left in UK!! Eventually picked up by Celestine, my sister-in-law, arrived home after midnight!! A bumpy, darkened ride down the Mombasa road to South 'C', warm welcome from my little Kenyan family, hastily bolted down pilau and hit the sack. Slept soundly and awoke to a grey winter's morning. Went for a day out in downtown Nairobi—spent pleasant time walking around, absorbing all the sights and sounds of a new world. After lunch in the Kenyatta Conference Centre, we took a matatu—(matatu = Kenyan minibus: a form of transport ubiquitous to the Kenyan)—to Nairobi Safari Park animal sanctuary—saw lions, leopards, monkeys, hyena, cheetah, ostrich—lovely, lovely place, which served to whet my appetite for seeing these majestic animals in their natural habitat.

Sunday 27th July 2008

Brrr . . . Kenyan winter—a cool, grey morning. Sat, without ceremony, on the edge of my bed, niece Mimi preparing for Uni. exams in the living room, Terri (my wife) getting up eventually, showering, dressing in my midst. Need to think about picking up the rest of our luggage from the airport this morning. Can't wait to get out of town and start exploring the country.

What a great day!! Got a phone call from the airport—our bags have finally arrived—went off with L. (niece #2) in a taxi to collect at Jomo—the taxi was falling apart (literally); the exhaust was shot and the fumes practically asphyxiated us! Having pulled the taxi over, the police spoke to L. in Swahili—she later told me that they "advised her to tell the taxi driver to change his tyres!" Nevertheless, was very happy to be reconnected with our luggage at last—having worn the same garments for almost 3 days, was extremely happy for a fresh shirt.

L. and I then went down into town for the afternoon—it was wonderful, we checked out the Kenya National Archive and beheld amazing artifacts—weapons, tribal masks, sculptures, paintings and photographs documenting Kenyan history over the last 150 years; after, we went to Java Coffee house, had a great lunch and caught a matatu back home—L. is sweet, pretty, intelligent and great company—I made a special friend today!!

Monday 28th July 2008

Into Nairobi—Westlands ~ the 'Chelsea of Nairobi', rented Toyota 4x4, ate *'choma'*: (Bar-b-q-ed meat—ubiquitous Kenyan fare)

Tuesday 29th July 2008

SAFARI begins . . .

Nairobi ~ Emali ~ Amboseli National Park (Kilimanjaro):

A six-hour bone-shaking drive through bush country. Sighted wild, rambling zebra, ostrich, giraffe and a *huge* rogue elephant that had us sitting very quietly in our motor with the engine switched off as he made his way majestically, imperiously across the road in front of us.

Wednesday 30th July 2008
Amboseli ~ Tsavo West National Park ~ Voi

~ RIFT VALLEY PROVINCE ~

At last, animals—wild, in their natural habitat: lions, hippos, giraffe, dikdik, ostrich, elephants, wildebeest, buffalo, zebra, gazelle, hyena and impala: the beauty of Kilimanjaro and the Massai (altho' never saw the mountain, as covered in clouds!!)

Stayed the night at the furiously expensive but awesomely luxurious Ol-tukai Lodge, bang in the heart of the park at the base of Kilimanjaro, surrounded by nature in its purity: swamp, march, papyrus bog, woodland scrubs and scattered trees, boreholes and Massai homesteads. That evening, I jammed with the resident local musician and bought him a few beers.

Headed across Lake Amboseli, flat, white, salty and dried out; the next morning we drove out, escorted by an armed guard, who accompanied us in our vehicle to the edges of Tsavo West (more for show than safety, I feel). We then drove through Tsavo West and visited the amazing and unexpected Mzima springs, watched lazy hippos enjoying an afternoon bathe and watched out for crocs, which mercifully did not appear!!

Thursday 31st July 2008
Africa

oh wondrous continent!
today I drink deeply of your beauty.
my cup runs over,
red ochre subsuming my will.

gladness of heart,
joy and gratitude abundant.
deep in the visceral womb
of this gentle cradle of red earth,

I open my heart, my soul unlocked;
I flow freely along with the natural breath of life.
golden light dispels demons of slumber.

awakened, I tread lightly, joyfully
over warm sand that caresses
the soles of my feet.

I seek nothing 'cept
to breath in your blessings.

Voi

the natural rhythm
of early morning function
engenders feelings
of belonging and grace.

gentle folk, following their routines,
murmur greetings—
extending and
sharing warmth.

young school children
gaze in astonishment
and smile sweetly: "jambo muzungu!"

"jambo Kenya, I salute your longevity,
your grace and beauty."

I die each moment into your arms
and hope beyond hope to merge seamlessly
into the depths of your innate wisdom
and eternal understanding.

Monday 4th August 2008

So much has happened since last entry:

Arrived in Mombasa—funky little island city with all the expected delights—sights, sounds, smells, tastes—we found a brilliant Swahili eatery—the most delicious freshwater fish (Tilapia) and rice. Mmm, mouth-watering!

Then on down the 'south coast'—missed Diani beach by (well) about 60 km!! Ended up close to Lunga Lunga—Tanzanian border!! Eventually found our way back to Ukunda and settled into a cheap apartment to our liking—about 2000 shillings per night, with swimming pool! Alexis is in her element, spends all day every day in there.

I had my 'Mr. Bean moment' on finally locating the beach (well hidden and totally obscured from the road) and glorious Indian Ocean. Ahh, la mer!!!

Finally, a tropical paradise—it IS everything it is cracked up to be: warm sea, white sandy beaches, unspoiled by either development or developers, coconut palms litter the shoreline—every morning I make my way down there for meditation and a glorious swim.

Settle into a lazee holiday routine—early morning walk to the beach, back to base for breakfast, usually into Mombasa for lunch at 'AP Swahili House'—crossing the estuary on that crazee ferry. Ahhh!

Tuesday 5th August 2008
Spiked by Indian

sea urchins pounce,
an ocean that seeks retribution
for pleasures gleaned.

iridescent turquoise saltiness
remains a febrile memory.

glorious tepid water
that entices amnesia
of all in life that is troubling,
an endless vista of green,
rolling waves beckons
further voyage,

out, out, out, to coral reefs
that thunder gently, ominously
in the distance,

lying on my back in shallow waters,
the ocean's debris close neighbours
to my dreams,

floating aimlessly in star-shaped circles,
life comes to a standstill
and I am satiated ~
destination heaven.

Wednesday 6th August 2008
Miritini

the merest glance
into a crowded downtown café
sparks an adventure of
unparalleled charm.

old friends meet, lives lived apart,
the warmth of recognition
suffuses and envelops both
families with joy and happiness.

an invitation eagerly accepted
to visit a regular suburb of this
ramshackle mombasan world.

oh! glorious continent!
I take a stroll out of town;
the balmy afternoon breeze
takes the edge off a vacant heat.

past local townsfolk, who
acknowledge this apparition: a 'muzungu',
yet fellow traveler ne'er the less,
strolling backwards through time.

the azure blue of a cheery sky
meets red ochre earth at
a green, tree-spiked horizon
of gently rolling hills.

I amble down to a fertile coconut grove
that, from a distance appears deserted
yet, upon arrival is a hive of activity.

It is only the women who toil
in the baking afternoon sun,
washing clothes in a stream,
digging into the red soil,
sifting piles into smooth cones,
ready for brick construction.

tiny children crocodile walk through tall mangroves,
gaily chattering, briefly pausing
to greet this clumsy, ambling stranger:
"jambo jambo!".

I push on, past hidden homesteads—
a village, out of sight and
slumbering peacefully
in the warm afternoons embrace.

so this is how the old world was,
eternally reposing without intent,
basking in timeless tranquility.

gatherers, embarking upon simple tasks
to carry life's momentum irrevocably forward.

just to dwell in this enduring landscape
amongst regular folk
has induced a peaceful harmony
that will remain forever imprinted
upon my soul.

Saturday 9th August 2008

To the mountains.

Arrived at Djambini at about 4:30pm and checked into Gimwa Rest Lodge.

Nairobi ~ Naivasha ~ North Kinangop ~ Djambini.

This has been a memorable Saturday! From trip into town with Lynnet, picking up bits and pieces for my safari, finding the place to catch the matatu, yes, even the perennial runs!

The drive from Nairobi centre, past Westlands, climbing up, up and eventually a spectacular view across the Rift Valley, although pretty misty, got a glimpse of its majesty!

Arrival and quick departure from Naivasha—a bustling and noisy shantytown, if I ever saw one.

A splendid climb up to corner of the Abedares and then dropped off at North Kinangop, very similar to a Wild West frontier town. Felt a bit endangered as extremely rough looking customers abounded there (this is unabashed Kikuyu territory, site of the recent 'troubles')—awaited another matatu bound for Djambini—but this was a rogue and soon left this bunch of guys in the hands of the police, who had apprehended and handcuffed one of the crew—I had already formed suspicions when the cab took a wrong turn.

I alighted and started walking in the opposite direction, having been assured this was the route to Djambini.

Walked on for about an hour through ramshackle countryside, people tilling the fields, a wonderful set of virgin forest mountains on the left hand side—children calling out and giggling.

Hitched a ride into the next town where I picked up a matatu to where I am now spending the night.

3 cups of 'porridge' (Kenyan tea, for which I am beginning to acquire a taste) and a delicious plate of rice and vegetables later, I am cozily ensconced in my hotel room (500/—= £4) ready for my bed and wondering of the morrow—have set myself a 30km hike through wild jungle tomorrow—hope I make it!

'Second Sunday in August' ~ 10/08/08
Djambini ~ Gattaka-ini ~Thika

6 hour walk : 30 km!! Wow, have never been so exhausted, a six-hour trek through jungle—started off at 7:30am, lovely early morning, a deep blue sky, rural bliss, mountains nestling in the north east, Rift Valley spreading out south west.

A hasty egg, toast and *'chai'* and off I trundled.

When asked by a local resident where I was headed, I said "Gattaka-ini." "Vehicle?" "On foot," I said, miming walking with my fingers. His eyes widened, "you know, plenty elephant and other wild animal there!" I shrugged my shoulders, "I'll be okay!"

Nevertheless, was seriously nervous when I hit the jungle, squeezing myself precariously through an electronic fence into no-mans land.

I considered my options when I had caught a whiff of the rank wilderness and smell of elephant dung. Not one to back down, I swallowed my fear and marched on.

Clear evidence of recent elephant spoor lying all over the track, plus many broken trees, especially bamboo.

Finally came across a footprint, fresh in the mud—absolutely enormous!!

I continued on, listening with painstaking precision for sound of elephant in the mass of green jungle pushing into the cleared path—decided it is in God's hands and to accept my fate, whatever; besides, elephants are not carnivores and I'm a friendly sort of bloke!!

Many hours later, reached signs of human habitation, which was a blessed relief ~ I grabbed some transport one way and another to Thika, of literary fame.

Not overly impressed here in Thika—real dirty—got a room which was a pit, really noisy, smelly and filthy. Nevertheless, took a well-needed shower (cold), freshened up and went for a mosey. Do NOT find the locals (Kikuyu) very friendly or warm and they tend to laugh at me—ate a nondescript plate of chicken and chips in a darkened café and then looked around for a better place to stay—eventually settled on the 'December Hotel', formerly a grand place (built in 1963 and opened by Kenyatta himself), now completely run to seed.

Still, the better of 2 options; rested my weary bones and looked in alarm at a blackening big toe (right), hit the sack extremely early—about 7pm—but slept fitfully and eventually awoke around midnight, bathed, sat and settled back into another (more comfortable) bed.

Adventures over, I feel tremendously lucky to have got through the past 48 hours in one piece—bandits/wild elephant/etc. This has been a *fantastic*, memorable weekend, one that will live with me for many moons, as I remember my little safari amongst the real, off the beaten track, Kenyan world.

Friday 15th August 2008
Mombasa

behold! the sharpness, intensity and clarity
of our golden glowing globe,
occasionally obscured by winter clouds.

heat penetrates body,
a call to prayer penetrates mind,
hot dusty breaths coalesce with
the romance of the yonder,
unimagined: here and now!

the chaotic, the innocent,
the corrupt, the seductive,
the oppressive, the mayhem,
merge deliciously, uncomprehendingly
in an 'otherly-world' beauty
that bombards my spirit all at once
with tears of joy and sorrow.

ahh!! you crazy, gorgeous,
maddening holy city on
this sun-kissed corner of
Indian ocean,

how I relish this momentary submergence
into the bowels of your mystery and delight!

coming home to this ancient birth of cities,
a re-acquaintance with
open spirits of incomprehension,
of togetherness,

I breathe deeply of your eternal scramble for survival
in a conspicuously ephemeral
and dangerous dance
of life, hunger love and death.

Tuesday 19th August 2008

and last, but not least:

Today was just memorable—a number of 'firsts' that will forever remain etched in my memory bank.

Early start, stroll down to Diani beach, meditation alongside the gentle roar of the ocean—monkeys and a variety of tropical birds plying their morning chorus; the usual retinue of young guys, some picking shells, corals from the beach, others early-morning jogging, some practicing their gymnastics, cart wheeling, back somersaults etc. Very few bother with me now. 'Jambo papa!' is the most I get.

Chatting to a couple of guys and gals; Irene, a Luo lass from Kisumi, pretty as a picture, offering 'massage', which I gently declined, chatted away about her life and family.

Tobias, from Tanzania, his family refugees from Mozambique (everyone has a story to tell), offers to take me out to the coral reef (about 2km out to sea). I accept and agree to meet at 10ish.

Then back to the apartment for breakfast. Littl'un already in the pool, splashing gaily in the bright early morning sunshine.

Back to the ocean and Tobias punts me out to sea in a wonderfully ancient and decrepit dugout mango tree canoe with stabilizers, gliding gently out to the reef.

I don a pair of goggles and a snorkel and spend the next hour in delightful abandon, gazing in wonderment at the amazing spectacle that is the coral reef; a new world of such splendour and intrigue—purple, green and yellow coral and all manner of sponge, lichen and sea life glisten and sparkle before me. Shoals of wonderful, bizarrely coloured tropical fish queue up behind me accompanying me on my travels, gently nipping my legs when I stand up to clear my mask.

I spy lobster, a stripy sea snake, star fish—bright red and a infinitely varied assortment of shellfish. I could have floated all day in this undersea paradise.

Further, went strolling along an isolated sandbank, picking up multicoloured shells and coral—a slow punt back to the beach, iridescent blue-green water, the sun sparkling off a tepid sea, gentle thunder of surf, palms swaying peaceably, naturally, along mile after mile of white sands, a moment of sublime perfection and satisfaction that lives on and on.

In the late afternoon, I pointed the 4 x 4 down the road to the Tanzanian border and drove down to Lunga Lunga, my 'eldorado'—a great drive through lush equatorial bush, through vibrant, peaceful and colourful villages all the way to the border, gently rolling hills encompassing the landscape—
Riding back to Ukunda in the gathering dusk, all the majesty and beauty of sub-tropical Africa unfolded before my eyes and I realized a love and deep connection with this ancient and splendid continent.
As the sun gradually sank beneath the horizon, all the depth and subtlety of the diminishing light infused the scenery with such intensity; my breath quickened and I felt myself immersed and allied with this place as only I have felt on two other occasions—once in the Sahara, south of the Atlas mountains in Ouazazarte, Maroc and secondly in Gosainkund, Nepal, early morning in the Himalayas.

These rare moments confirm in my heart the reality of the Divine in the mundane.

~ with bows, 20th August 2008 ~

Diary—Christmas 2008 in Provence
23/12/08:

Sitting here in Aix—"chez Annie", having digested a delightful spinach quiche, salad and a demi-carafe of local red—the missus and littl'un having just popped out to buy a gift for Annie's (proprietress) daughter Chloe who has recently given birth to her first child.

Sitting here in Provence—mid-winter, bright, bright sunlight and a sky of immeasurably delightful deep, azure blue.

This place has character, class, beauty and finesse. There is something uniquely fine and uplifting about this part of the world. A combination of perfect climate—evergreen vegetation which matches its summer splendour, now in the depth of winter; the affable busyness and laid-back intensity of local shoppers, yet always the time to pass the time of day with friends and acquaintances—a chat, a shared laugh, *baisers* on both cheeks and on to the next assignment.

The musical brogue of Southern French mingles gracefully with the buzzing/farting 2-stroke engines of mopeds busying around ancient, narrow cobbled streets like worker bees. The ancient stone of the hills, crowded out by all manner of vine and deciduous branch; eternal amber sunlight highlighting the multi-coloured and fine architecture that heralds an ancient Mediterranean world of civility, timelessness and endearing, noble proportion of design.

Awakening this morning after a 14-hour drive across this vast country—from a limpid London, foggy and tired in its pre-dawn somnambulance.

8am: Throwing open the pea-green shutters at Roumanille: a gasp of wonderment at an impeccably pristine clarity of azure blue, gently tapering into a velvet orange at the merging of sky with distant mountain, inhaling a pure nectar of pine-filled scent that courses through body and enthralls the spirit.

A timeless and ecstatic moment of connection with mother earth in transcendent intimacy and supplicative will. I have come home again. *Déjà vu, toujours vu.*

25/12/08: Christmas day:

The day broke—grey damp and cold: extraordinary how we apply our perceptions onto our lives—the world, neutral, as it was, is and always will be:—manifesting just as it is.

Our shifting ambience, moods, perceptions and feelings—these are constantly changing and directly affect what appears 'out there.'

How wonderful to rise early, here, in the verdant foothills of the Alps; magnificent and arousing scent of pine and the gentle breath of wilderness cascading through our senses.

The overwhelming peace and noiseless impeccability of the countryside seeps into my ethereal, tired body.

I take a deep breath as I sit on mottled pink slabs of the living room floor; having forgotten to pack my zafu and zabuton (sitting cushion and mat), I make do with local bench seat cushions; I breath in deeply and expel air. Adjust my posture, straighten my back, tuck chin in, lower eyelids and gaze into whitewashed wall.

Gradually all aches and pains and mental anxieties subside, I observe my thoughts, taking me back, *back, am now 3-years-old, it is Xmas in '55, I toddle into the dining room—Santa's grotto sparkling in the fireplace, it is very cold, snowing and white outside, a sharp greyness abounds—there waiting for me is a huge, shiny red pedal car, as real as real can be; delight, excitement grabs me.*

The image fades, now back to the present. I observe myself merging into the eternal present moment—a wondrous sense of intimacy envelopes my world and I feel a huge and strong correspondence with all of existence; I feel peace and a strange, dislocated joy; aware of the limited span of my current frame, nevertheless I give thanks for the grace of consciousness.

The world of human awareness is a continuous cycle of events repeating themselves endlessly with variation over the span of individual and collective lifetimes.

Another moment, another day, another Christmas, just like the last one, yet entirely different—new, yet old, close at home, yet estranged from, understood yet mysterious.

The great dilemma that is our birthright continues unabated despite our leanings and imaginings—as it was, is and will be. I give thanks for the beneficent birth of Jesus, a true Bodhisattva who has brought so much love into our world, peace to him and all mankind.

Sat 27/12/08

Upon awakening this morning, I cast a lingering glance out of our first floor bedroom window. Our rustic hideaway affords a wonderful view across a wide valley, perched as it is, on the side of the Grand Luberon, a vast horizontal foothill here in the mountains. Gazing across this beautiful wilderness of pure forest, ancient grey and brown hills and rock buttresses, the horizon was suffused with brilliant early morning illumination.

The sky, mainly overcast with grey impenetrable cloud, was broken at the horizon's edge. The sun, rising, threw out a golden glow of great intensity that lit up everything and transformed the world with a mass of vibrant hues and colour. My spirits lifted, as the last couple of days have been sunless. As I prepared to sit, my soul seemed to sing with joy, immersed as it was with this golden energy.

It is extraordinary how the light of the sun can affect our mood and bequeaths a truly appropriate metaphor for correspondence with our moods and feelings. As I sat, the sun, rising further, abounded this clear crack in the sky and very soon disappeared behind the grey blanket of cloud, hovering above.

Immediately the wall in front of me became quite dark and I felt an immediate correspondence of feeling from within. The dance of joy became subdued and an abject melancholy gripped my inner perception. The light went out; yet I have learned not to identify with these subtle changes of feeling and simply to observe the unfolding moment, and this is what I saw:

The reality of consciousness is not fixed and therein lies a great beauty, peace and constancy.

Changing irrevocably, the less we attach to this denouement, the more able are we to benefit from the fruits of detachment. Each moment brings with it clarity and freshness, it is only our clinging and fear that prevent us from basking in this reality; our judgmentalism that fixes the moment into a tired framework of either boredom, frustration, smugness or similar perception. The challenging task is remain open, honest and have the courage to let go of the familiar path; not easy and mostly downright inconvenient. The Dharma sets us straight and we need only trust in the truth that non-interference leads to awakening. The method is simple—a daily commitment to sitting still and letting go of our imagined control over our lives and unfolding histories.

Having arisen from my contemplation this morning, a mottled sky affords a gaily-changing carousel of light and dark to welcome in a new day of fun and delight.

• zen reflections

on silence

the beauty of silence is that I find it most powerful when I am surrounded by noise, if that is not too paradoxical. when I am sitting, especially early in the morning—[I rise at 4am and sit for 40 minutes before starting my day], it is quiet, peaceful—but in that space there is the sound of the body breathing, circulating blood, heart pumping, not least the thoughts that circumambulate one's brain endlessly. nevertheless within this cacophony there are glimpses of Silence that transcend the mundane and render all one's 'musings' to the recycling bin.

no, it is in the noise and confusion and desperate disorder of the morning commute, the rushing home of a hot summer's evening, surrounded in the underground by hot, dissatisfied, sweating and proximous bodies, that I find Silence amidst the chaos—this is the wondrous silence that transcends all understanding and rationality—that confounds and denies dissemination.

it is the Moment of the still, small voice that embraces one's poor soul and holds at bay the terrifying fears of annihilation and death that face us and emboldens us to walk forward in the knowledge that there is an Unborn, Undying, Uncreated that was, is and will forever hold us in Its embrace.

on the wondrous merit of 'anticipation'.

come to mind the wondrous benefits of ~ waiting; waiting for the unexpected to occur, waiting for the washing machine repairman to come—dreaming of fresh shirts to wear; waiting for a phone call from a loved one, waiting for the train to arrive—shivering in the early morning frost at your suburban train station; waiting for your name to be called at the doctors, waiting for the day to arise, early in the morning—wondering what the day will bring; waiting for the mail—that important document to arrive that will transform your fortunes; waiting for ~ whatever life's hand is to deal you.

on the wondrous merit of anticipation: for when we IMAGINE, the richness of our expectation far outweighs the tangible results. for whatever truly arrives, it will only be a poor approximation of the imagined joy that precedes the 'fait accompli.' indeed once the arrival manifests, it is back to the drawing board, onward to the next occurrence which once again we build up beyond realistic boundaries.

the bottom line is desire desire desire wants wants needs needs can't do without can't do without, if only if only, but for but for, et cetera . . .

one can learn to rest deeply and contentedly in the pool of anticipation, indeed to find Truth and Satisfaction in the not having, not receiving, not accomplished—for therein lies True Reality in which the ever present promises nothing but yields everything. oh to experience the true humility of unrequited love, the bliss of not quite reaching the mark, the joy of missing an important appointment, the ecstasy of misunderstanding—for in these disappointments lies the power of Imagination to supply and enrich the anticipatory musings the "there is always the future" . . . to beckon and impress the entrenched yearnings of the Heart Mind that is ever-present effervescent.

we will never achieve True satisfaction—this is what Life is Showing us, Teaching us to remain Grateful and Awed with the beauty of the Moment which is JUST AS IT IS. no frills attached.

each day that passes.

each day that passes brings me closer, closer to Life, closer to Awakening,

for I have that 'still small voice' to guide me at all times, through good times and bad, through temptation and the desperate effort to avoid succumbing.

no matter how hard we try we cannot avoid Reality for ever. all we need to do is to face up and brave the storm, the emptiness, the not knowing, the not understanding, the joy, the bliss, the pain, the anger, the fighting, the retaliative, and the brick wall of our stubbornness.

oftwhile I feel blessed, I feel blessed, I feel cursed—always it is my febrile self that is making these assumptions—need only to bow deeply and accept that Life will show us the Truth—the eternal way is laid out before me without deceit or chicanery—it is no easy matter/it is an easy matter to strip away the illusion of self importance and allow the Eternal to manifest in which ever way it does at this very moment.

thank you Lord for granting me the gift of Life and the rare and unique ability to reflect on It's nature—I will forever bow down and give homage to this wondrous beneficence and will for eternity love you and die for you each minute, so that I may live with your Boundless glory in perpetuation, even when my 'little-self' rails and squirms to find its base gratifications and momentary thrills which pale into insignificance in the great Scheme of your infinite Blessings.

on conversion

life is full of surprises, one day is divorced entirely from the next and there is absolutely no guarantee of continuity whatsoever.

it is therefore of great value and importance NEVER to become too attached to any insight, mood, revelation and so on—likewise do not push away the 'malevolent', for therein lie teachings also—we cannot pretend to our Inner selves—the impulses that elbow their way to the surface have to be accepted and acknowledged—the Great Benefit is Not To Act On Them.

the great journey of which we are willing/unwilling passengers continues relentlessly and without pause, there is no disembarkation (until the final stop over which we have no control)—it is also of UTMOST importance and urgency to become fully alert and a committed participant in the unfolding drama—for let us be honest—THERE IS NO HIDING PLACE.

stand steadfast in the presence/glare of Consciousness—hold mind/body upright against the intemperate meanderings of circumstance and do your best to find Value and Goodness in all the vicissitudes that you encounter each moment.

on developing mindfulness

there is a tendency to focus on Mindfulness on the zafu (meditation cushion)—after all, that is why we are sitting in the first place, is it not? further, there is the ingrained inclination to come off of the cushion and 'snap' into 'normal thinking' mode—as if, in fact, the sitting is a separate activity.

my current continuing koan (metaphysical tester) is to learn to take this Mindfulness further each time; having arisen from the mat, continue to maintain awareness cultivated and nurtured so diligently through meditation.

there is struggle, frustration but joy and increasing confidence in this striving. i have noticed, for example the tiny details and subtleties that manifest in each movement and activity following on from 'arising from the mat'. it is a labour of love, really. continuously to bring yourself back once, ten times, hundreds of times, ten thousand times daily to the Present. okay what is really going on here? so easy to sneak by any unpleasantness, any slight irritation—gloss over malicious thoughts "'look at the state of so and so, glad that is not me'" and so on. the Right way is to stop the autopilot, look into the motivation for that thought and however excruciating and painful it may seem, let the resolution come, let it go and perform the next act of examination/exhumation that will present itself very shortly. all of this and of course daily living in the world with all of its hustle, bustle, non-sequitors, contact, agreement, disagreement, brick walls, flow and so on.

who said it was going to be easy? but there again—pause for a moment; check out that sky above the skyline to the West—you will never see that configuration again. never, ever. and yet. and yet, it grows on you.

enjoy the rest of the day. enjoy the rest of your life. be brave, warrior like. do not be a worrier.

sufficient unto the day thereof

hold on! there is no merit in contemplating what may or may not occur in an unknown, unsolicited, unbeckoned future. for the exemplar way is to hold fast to ~ NOW. **this** is when It is occurring, **this** is what is important, **this** is what is happening, all the rest is but a dream, a fantasy, a "maybe," a "could happen," a "what if," an "if only,"

why oh why do we refuse to see what is here?!
do we really imagine we can avoid It?
do we truly believe in our idle meanderings?
can we not feel the hearty slap in the face of unambiguous Truth that is lying in wait?

it is no trap, friends, It is ubiquitous and truly our only ally from hereon in, let us vow to open our Hearts and welcome home this long lost, ever present, omniscient and bountiful, beautiful Presence that is beckoning us without calling—that is screaming gently in the Silence.

thank you Consciousness for parting the waves of disbelief and opening the gateless gate of wonder/awe/joy/gratitude.

I will forever hereon listen to your still small voice.

on facing our 'Karma'

how very complex and challenging it is to 'get to grips' with our personal karma.

every breath we take, every action we make is firmly embedded in our personal journey through our lifetime(s.)

I know, for myself, I have many, many, myriad issues that lie in wait, unresolved, and accumulated over immeasurable eons.

how on earth am I able to cope with these, to deal with these?
the truth is manifest every time these accumulations arise and we are unable to comprehend our reactions, emotions, responses to the unimpeachable unfolding of our personal destinies.

for despite our best efforts, we will forever be unable to comprehend the vastness of this enterprise, but, [and this is a tiny chink of supreme light amidst the darkness of our ignorance]—BUT there is a 'method' we can apply to enable a just and equitable response and resolution to these grave matters.

the simple answer is to sit still within the temple of our consciousness, there must be Faith, Trust and Determination to see this through; despite the enormity of the task, despite the hopelessness of the cause—there has to be RESOLVE of the highest order.

never, ever imagine that you will see the Biggest picture but nevertheless we can adopt an Attitude of Humility. In this endeavour, a wealth of beneficence will come our way.

simply by accepting our powerlessness to alter the passage of our karma and facing unflinchingly the phenomena that manifest as feelings, dread, terror and more, will we by our courage TRANSFORM our Understanding and aspirations (and hence our fortunes.)

the Dharma has a beautiful applet ~ Sange (contrition) is the 'élan vital'—that method by which we can move forward sure-footedly and harmoniously and fear not to tread forth and live fulfilled lives.

whilst the world sleeps

whilst the world sleeps, I raise my trembling eyelids aloft and gaze with immaculate humility at the unfolding azure of the morning sunrise.

my first thought is one of gratitude. the immediate and present knowledge of the unconditional blessings of Awareness, Equanimity and Beneficence flood through my consciousness like a tsunami of Light and Joy.

i raise my weary body from its horizontal mien and immediately raise my hands in gassho as a way of acknowledging my return.

i spring light heartedly forth to greet the pre-prandial hours with determination, resolution and a peppering of wonder.

without the merest glance back, i post myself on the mat after morning ablution, banish acatalepsy from my vision and open my heart and mind to the abode of the Buddha.

i become released from life and death and throw my life toward Unconditioned Awakening.

welcome oh new day, whilst the world sleeps, i awaken.

baking bread as a metaphor for living

it strikes me that the process of baking bread is an apposite metaphor for describing the essential elements of living.

what is the first ingredient needed? right intention—we eat to live; we eat food that is natural and a product of natural growth: flour, honey, yeast, water (a touch of salt.)

what is the motivation? we eat to live—we love to provide sustenance for our selves and our loved ones.

what is the process?—the process is as old as life itself—the method is as old as the history of humankind—chuck a few natural blessed elements together in a bowl, allow time to gel together, bake the amalgam in a hot oven, then, simply, eat, enjoy, be sustained.

i make bread every week and have done for over thirty years. each loaf is different, yet the same. many times things have gone wrong, many times things have not worked to plan—yet each loaf has provided sustenance and providence for those who have done the eating.

i did not create the ingredients, but merely fashioned my knowledge and understanding to put them together in the right proportions and in the right sequence; over the years i have perfected my technique and, when all the elements are right, the end product is wonderful and tasty and life-sustaining.

of course, the essential element is right mindfulness: if i make it all with as much Presence and Love as i can muster, then the end product is as delicious as any earth food can possibly be.

i give thanks and gratitude to all who came before me and passed on this wondrous art and to the bountiful Earth and Sun for providing the right ingredients to allow this weekly act of thanks giving to unfold with joy and peace.

on leaving for the temple

tomorrow morning, very early, i leave home for the temple.

i will be spending a week reaffirming my commitment to following the Buddhist Way. i will be attending Jukai (the taking of the Precepts ~ lay ordination).

i first attended Jukai in September 1978, when i joined the bloodline of the Soto Zen community.

i reaffirmed my commitment again in April 2003.

this will be my third attendance at the Jukai ceremony and i am thoroughly looking forward to it.

i hope to experience a joyous confirmation of Beneficence and Togetherness, which is something that follows me daily in tandem with my ordinary life.

Jukai diary

Sat 7th April

arrive at the temple, Throssel Hole Buddhist Abbey, in Northumberland—settle in.

Sun 8th April

hard going! usual physical pain, sitting—seems much harder arising after each meditation period than ever before—severe pain in ankles etc.

a glimmer. need to stick with it; don't push anything away. having said that, slept through the majority of last meditation period!

evening: had a sudden desire to quit—felt disillusioned with the general hustle and bustle and in my mind decided to leave in the morning. sat through Reverend Master (RM) D.'s reading of the Kyojukaimon in a bit of a strop!
nevertheless, enjoyed and gave full attention to 'Sange'—which was cleansing and sharp.
after vespers, i had a word with Rev. L. (guest master) and relayed to her my intention to quit the sesshin—just felt in need of rest and felt the Jukai week extremely demanding etc, and too much for me at present. she showed concern and understanding, asked me to 'sleep on it' and make a decision in the morning.

Mon 9th April

having 'slept on it', i have resolved to see the week through; having made the commitment, i feel honour bound to stick to it, despite my reservations.

i really came awake during the morning meditation and feel i am beginning to get centred, grounded and focused.
i relayed my decision to carry on to the monks and they urged me to 'look after myself' and rest as much as i wanted to—this was gratefully received.
consequently, i excused myself from the morning working meditation period and am enjoying this time to rest and contemplate.

pm: most excellent Dharma talk by RM—talked about the operation of Sange and how important and valuable it is to accept our anger, greed and delusion and see beyond to what out True Nature is.

followed by a most beneficial and peaceful zazen (sitting meditation); beginning to get a really good feel for this retreat. so glad i decided to stay.

ahhh dear!! Rev. A.'s Dharma talk was brilliant—an old man with a terminal illness—but such humility, humour and indeed wisdom and insight—i love him!

was server at mealtimes today—made a bit of a pig's ear of it at medicine meal, but okay at breakfast and lunch—mistakes taken with a pinch of humour!

the sesshin is really progressing—an okay bunch of people and a few laughs in amongst the 'serious' issues.

Tues 10th April

tired—but i feel a spring in my step and my mischievous humour returning! somehow difficult to describe, feel a qualitative difference in perception—a lightness, a freshness and a brightness—i glide effortlessly between activities and am able to be fully present at every moment of every activity.

a somewhat grey day ensued—a day devoted to the Sange ceremony and therefore focusing on the 'to-be-ordained' trainees—an enigmatic Dharma talk by RM Daishin this morning—

many people feel the need to try and interpret his talk from an intellectual/ rational perspective—this will not work—you have to suspend intellectual judgment and listen with the heart for the Truth to penetrate.

a restful afternoon spent sleeping and reading.

Wed 11th April

last night's Sange ceremony was awesome—these guys sure know how to put on a show!—as good as anything on broadway!

more to the point, the Sange ceremony allows you to truly reflect on your confession and contrition and has the wondrous power to completely cleanse you of all previous karma—"Namu Shakyamuni Buddha"

this morning, first meditation was truly inspiring—complete calm, peace, joy and a condition of Awakening!
this spot is truly blessed—bang in the middle of the North Pennine Way and totally natural and quiet. this is truly my home from home and will always be so.

wonderful wonderful day—what more can i say? sitting was hard—afternoon seemed painful and fruitless ~ beautiful spring evening, quiet, majestic, PEACEFUL, glorious as only the deep countryside can be—evening zazen was an absolute delight—did not want it to end, EVER!! felt truly awake, alive and blissful—thank you Life for granting me these moments of wonder. the key is: open your heart fully—just be totally open to what is presented—do not judge, discriminate, grasp or reject any nuance, just be open open open and lo and behold IT speaks.

Thur 12th April

woke up in the middle of the night sweating and scared—had escaped from a seriously frightening dream ~ of 'hell'—indeed i was in hell in this dream and unimaginable terrors, apparitions and atrocities were happening or being performed—it was so real as to be monumentally awesome.

on awaking in the depths of darkness i found myself calling upon RM Jiyu for comfort and refuge—i also began to chant 'Namu Shakyamuni Buddha' and holding my hands in mudra. this was immediately beneficial and i soon felt calm and safe and the darkness no longer held any fear whatsoever for me.

i have always fallen prey to extreme fear at night in the temple. i believe it is through intensive sitting over a sustained period of time (7-8 hours per day): we open ourselves up to all manner of Beings—we become vulnerable in our openness and must attract the hungry ghosts et al.

faith protects us, though, if we are truly committed—nothing can harm us.

today appeared in beauteous bountiful spring-like paradise. sun cascading over the purple and green hills and valleys, smell of heather and country perfumes wafting in the breeze—incessant chattering of birds and other country animals murmuring satisfaction in the spring light.

not a lot to say about today really, business as usual, moments of inspiration/ insight, plenty of sitting, moments of reflection and déjà vu—one must learn to give up expectations: things are never the same twice; keep reminding myself to be OPEN—simple, really.

Fri 13th April

final full day of retreat—tonight's ceremony is Recognition. Buddha recognises Buddha! the question is: how awake are we? hopefully this week has reinforced an established pattern of action—provided a Stillness and a recognition of the transitory nature of our lives—most importantly though it has reaffirmed my commitment to live my life in Truth: i have thankfully at my disposal a Golden method of maintaining the best possible attitude and engaging in a process towards this goal: Zazen; Serene Reflection Meditation. for this i am eternally grateful.

Homage to the Buddha, Homage to the Dharma, Homage to the Sangha.

postscript: at last!! just sitting on a quiet and peaceful spring afternoon—no big deal, just sitting; no other agenda whatsoever.

Dogen in the playground

balmy spring saturday afternoon,

accompany Alexis to the local playground,

she meets a friend Ballu ~ entreaties for money to buy ice cream,

me, dad, sitting reading Shobogenzo, such sweet transmission,

huge sycamore swaying gently in the breeze. enlightenment was, is and will

always be parallel with the moment, there is nothing more than This,

entreaties from the girls to go home to play with their toys,

sure, I'm easy, there is after all nothing else to do.

on 'getting what we need'

it often strikes me, we don't always get what we want, but we always get what we need.

this 'i' that we carry with us, that at times we cherish, at others we try (erroneously) to distance ourselves from is truly worth close investigation,

however, it is the manner of investigation that determines whether we come to a true, enlightened understanding of its nature, or whether we simply bolster, shore up and celebrate a false sense of pride, ownership and indeed arrogance.

[believe me, the distance between these two opposing perspectives is as minute as a grain of sand and immense as a cluster of galaxies.]

it is indeed a complex conundrum, this 'i' this 'me' this little self—it clings to our attention like a motherless child that seduces us and convinces us that the answer to all desires lies in their immediate gratification.

it charms us into believing that all we feel, all we know is as a result of its immense wisdom and clarity.
it promises us delight, satiation and a sense of repletion.
and yet, and yet is it not true that, no matter how often we allow ourselves to fall prey to its siren-like manifestations, somehow, in some way, it is never enough. not quite, almost. just for a second we are replete and satisfied; but oh, how short the moment is. before we know it, we want the next thing and the next, ad infinitum, how boring, how frustrating this becomes.

there is another way, believe me.

across that minute grain of sand, astride those myriad galaxies lies a True path.

it is not little me who discovered it—but i have been fortunate and blessed to have been shown the way by the wondrous and impeccable art of Meditation which is our birthright and rests with us aware or unaware, awake or asleep, alive or dead.

the first rule is ~ surrender ~ we must be prepared to give up all our intellectual knowledge and beliefs, these simply obstruct our true awareness and will forever prevent us from discovering the unsurpassable and unimpeachable emptiness that lies at the heart of all existence.

this will come easily to those of us who have reached the limits of our little minds and found our endless desires unfulfilled.

on the verge of awakening

isn't it truly amazing how people meet, collide and become friends, across continents, different worlds, different lives, and different times. and yet, and yet, correspondence, united in this amazing journey of life, this difficult, unfathomable, outrageous, inexplicable and yet beautiful, limitless and wondrous panorama of feeling and experience.

whilst you are dreaming right now it is early morning on this side of the pond and I have just arisen from my morning Sitting.

things quite hard at the moment, life throwing challenges and trials my way, but thankfully am able to offer up all my woes and worries to the 'Sunyata'—[Emptiness] that is before me when i sit.

'emptiness' is a strange but accurate and time-honoured way of describing the awakened state that is the essence of Zazen [a.k.a. serene reflection meditation—let's just call it 'Sitting'.]

well, that IS the essence of Sitting—to quieten the mind and allow the incredible reality that is the Awakened state to show itself without the hindrance and judgmentalism of our intellect trying to direct the course of our understanding.

the secret with correct sitting is to ~ just sit. with no agenda other than to spend the next 35 minutes allowing everything to settle down. just watch carefully what is going on in your mind—do not try to direct your thoughts. do not follow your thoughts, just notice them and allow them to pass across your mind. do not hold on to them, do not push them away. no grasping, no avoiding. just watch, listen—the Truth will arise naturally, that i can assure you . . .

you will find at first that your mind is so so busy and crowded—that's okay that's cool—what is happening is that you are beginning to notice at a deeper level—bit by bit the busyness will disappear, for when you stop feeding and following your thoughts, they will dry up . . . and THEN, oh boy, you will get it!! a moment of bliss and serene reflective quiet that is indescribable but oh so real that it will guide you for eternity.

run while you have the light of life

recently came across a brilliant piece of writing which introduced me to the
'Rule of St. Benedict'.
what leapt off of the pages and hit me with great force was the synchronicity
of his vision to that of Buddhism! [and, I guess, the root of all spiritual
traditions.]

St Benedict was a sixth century monk of the Christian faith:

* **Stability**—<suscipe me>—'accept me O Lord as I am'
accepting myself and refusing to run away from myself is in essence what the
vow of stability is all about.

* **Conversion**—<conversation morum>—continual conversion to life
it means living open to change.

* **Obedience**—<listening>
listening in its fullest sense; listening with every fibre of my being; hearing
and responding to that still, small voice.

i could wax lyrical on these matters, but, dear reader, i will leave the digestion
to you to perceive the dynamic that underlies these profound thoughts.

with bows and gratitude.

starting afresh

tomorrow is a new day. a new dawn—a new beginning.

everything we have learned to date is of no import. we must view the enlightening of the day with beginner's eyes.

we must marvel at the freshness of colour, the lightness of sound, the depth of feeling. we must adopt a naive and uncompromising attitude to all we encounter.

we must praise every unfolding moment. we must ask for continuing support from our intuition to guide us effortlessly through the electric ether.

we must not hurry—we must not become impatient; we will welcome distraction and peer closely at the edges of things.

we will not seek fulfillment, nor will we shrug off understanding. we will explore with vigour and delight every nuance, every possibility.

we will return again and again to the present moment; we will not give in to intolerance or boredom.

we will seek newness in the most travelled routes. we will not allow ourselves the dubious self-gratification of old.

we will grasp at straws, gather all wit and circumstance to our breast and praise Life for allowing us this Ultimate Freedom.

we will explore our limitations and gleefully surpass all previous barriers.

we will laugh in the face of adversity and gladly hand over power to the moment to unfold as it will.

we cannot change what is, what was, what will be, but we can open wholeheartedly to the infinite possibilities that did, do and will present Themselves.

we will live, in fullness.

on choice

mmm, 'choice' . . .

this is such a pivotal word and concept in and of the human experience.

implicit in this small, one syllable word is the crux, the core, the essential tool of homo sapiens.

for historically, in the beginning, choice was the 'God-given' prerogative of man. this ability was what separated man from his fellow sentient beings.

indeed, without the knowledge and ability to freely use our rationality to make decisions, we would be infinitely poorer within the panorama of our life experience.

is this not the Glory, the immense privilege we have been granted: minutely, hourly, daily to be face with the either/or, ideally the both and?

and how this was, is and will be abused by mankind; it is reckless—thoughtlessness. we will forever pay the price for unwise action. {give a beggar a horse and he will ride to hell.]

and yet, and yet, this is also our ultimate redemption; for we always have this ability to turn things around.

if we look deeply into the matter, this freedom we have been granted to choose at every point of our lives is what truly emancipates us and allows us ultimate True expression.

we will, if we allow our minds to settle and see through to the Peace beyond, always make the right choice, for in our hearts we KNOW what is the best thing to do—instinctively, beyond rationality, trustingly.

and this truly is our redemption.

we don't have to live in pain, fear and hopelessness.

we always had, have and will have that inner voice to guide us to wise action.

we know this to be true; it is not always easy to follow this path and allow Truth to manifest without egoistic interference; it is a long road of surrender, hope and faith.

but dear reader, i assure you this perpetual wise action is the route best followed—always choose the path of selflessness and the informed choice will lead you to the Treasure house and you will prevail.

'Hard It is to find,
the Truth no easy thing to know:
Craving is pierced by one who seeth,
no self remains, no earthly woes;
for him: eternal life, serene repose.'

with bows.

ahh! the bliss

ahhh, the bliss of trusting the Eternal to take care of all our pains, worries, fears, irritations, tiredness, aching limbs, frustrations, misunderstandings, mistakes, u-turns, failures.

the rush of gratitude when that crowded train pulls in and there is standing room only—at least it takes you one step further.

the thanklessness of being mown down by an irritable and over hasty commuter rushing to get a seat at the expense of another. Why thank you for awakening me, I was in a pre-weekend stupor and now fully aware of everything going on around me.

little one, tired from the week at school, crying copious tears at the injustice of her friends unprovoked attack on her neck.

aching feet on a weary frame stretched to its limits over a sustained work period; automatic plod of feet over unforgiving pavements, ready to trip up the unsuspecting traveler.

eventual collapse through the front door, mind whirling, images of great deeds performed through the week; the grateful smile of a colleague who loves you for your faithfulness, the hug from a pupil who loves you for you commitment and positive good regard.

the unfailing unflinching certainty that all is well with the world, despite the pain, the hurt, the heat the hardness of the city air pressing down on overcrowded brain.

and i lay it all down, spread it all under the omniscient, beneficent gaze of He Who Knows and willingly picks up the pieces as they fall off my life and hands them back, renewed, refreshed, reappraised, clean, sharp, new and pure.

the flip side

I guess the beauty of opening ourselves fully to what presents itself moment to moment is that, like fallen snow: which melts under the sun's glow, moods that are heavy and leaden—disappear only to leave no trace whatsoever, thankfully, after all, is not ceaseless change the only constant?

wondrously, yesterday's doldrums have dissipated!!

despite the sky falling in today and covering our velvet city with a blanket of wetness that snuffed out any possibility of outdoor activities, the day passed pleasantly.

idling away time,
pointedly, aimlessly,
wonderfully without goal or intent.

weekly chores dutifully performed,
baking, shopping, tidying, cleaning
then the fun begins,

teasing, cajoling playing endlessly
with happy-go-lucky seven year old
bundle-of-fun,

no chance of resting on any decision
the only rule—
have fun and laughter

this is bountiful, delicious happiness,

["Daddy, I never want to grow up to be an adult; I want now to last forever."

"Why darling, today is forever and never forget it,
we'll dance through eternity with lightness, love and happiness."]

and the bogeymen will forever stand, faces pressed against the glass, wishing they were us, don't you know!!

of many, making one

attending to the breath, i turn over recent events in my mind.

hard to believe the integrity of each living moment.

so fair, so fair. so kind, so kind; it is marvelously easy to be open to presence.

joy and gratitude spill from my pores like pure nectar; [hurt, indifference and coldness are unable to penetrate the inner core.]

and yet a vile week recedes in the rear-view mirror of my path through the month that is not summer.

so many challenges—so many little tests of character; a mere pawn in the Almighty's hands and yet such power, such opportunity to erase the pain and make manifest the virtue that lies waiting in every encounter.
let's laugh, after all, at the game!

yet deadly serious, costly and erroneous to mistake calculated indifference as hastening by un-noticed.

nothing escapes reflection, nothing escapes the present and all encompassing attention of the eternal moment.

and yet—'NO BLAME' must be our mantra.

we must give up all hope to achieve awakening; we cannot expect to get 'it' right.

to fully admit defeat is to broaden our compassion and be thus rightly placed to experience the thrill of the breath OF THE MOMENT.

for this breath, yes, this breath is the first breath we will ever take.

it may also be the last breath we ever make; how therefore can there be hope?

and yet is this not entirely liberating, for it allows us to embrace not-knowing, humility, wonder and the unsurpassable delight of the unknown, unencountered gifts of Life we have been granted.

i relish the paradox of the opposites, the frustration of not quite making it in the moment, for this is where our humanity thrives and flourishes; in the mistakes, in the false utterances—always the chance to make amends, always the path of forgiveness.

on change

this word is at the very heart, the very essence and inner core of life as we know it.
indeed it is so very central to every action, every motion and every step we take, that its significance becomes lost in ubiquity.
it is our greatest friend and at times, our most feared adversary.
for with change, breathes new life, freshness, a clearing of the decks.

also we fear change when the world, albeit temporarily, is 'just so'—and within a mere flash—gone is the moment of ecstasy, snatched from our grasp by the inevitability of movement, flux.

if we stay still, the character that exemplifies its shape can be a great illumination; for within the process lie all manner of teachings—it cannot, however be understood by the discriminatory mind.

within the process, lies eternally the opposite: where there is life, death; where there is light, darkness. Where there is growth, lay the seeds of decay. Where there is hope, therein also hides despair.
where there is pride, only hidden—failure.
but what a dreadful place this world would be if change did not rule supreme.

within the physicality of our offspring lie its beauty and genetic presence . . .
the future painted out in soft and vibrant hues that withhold doom and tragedy and produce gaiety and reflected glory.

the angry sky betrays a bounteous sun behinds its mask; the gruffness of an adult's scolding belies a warm and gentle embrace.

the terror of war eventually dissipates to reveal a mesmeric silence that lasts for an eternity; but there again eternity is above and beyond this hallowed ground.

within eternity's scope change has little currency—for riding above the warp and woof of earthly concerns lies a landscape of serenity and indifference.

it is only ours to grapple with, this change that lies at the heart of all our earthly meanderings. We can only rest assured that ultimately Transcendence sleeps curled up like an old friend at the door of Awakening.

we will eventually escape its inchoate clutches, but not before we have savoured its incredible detail, its seemingly random choices—the beauty and terror of the yet-to-be-faced, yet the marvelous unpredictability that lie at its heart—the knowing of the unknown.

as seeds grow

this life we share is remarkable. we must always bear this truth in the forefront of our minds. there is never a moment when we can afford to allow cynicism, despair and doubt to belittle our consciousness.

it is no easy matter to aspire to this truth; always the possibility of life's wayward path diverting us from the integrity of this discovery.

no easy thing to smile through misfortune, tragedy and disaster; it is so hard to let go of our standpoint and realisations, hard won. this however is a necessity, if we are to remain true to the Present, which is the only Truth that has meaning, reality and power.

as seeds grow, life reveals itself in all its mystery, depth and beauty.

as seeds grow, we can travel forward effortlessly, in the knowledge that there is no thing we can do, no thing we can accomplish without complete and utter trust in The Process.

as seeds grow, so too do we grow in stature, shedding our withered conceptions day by day, allowing truth to penetrate our hardened misunderstandings that stifle creativity, joy and movement.

to let go, open our hands, hearts and minds to the glory that is manifest endlessly, can we but see it, is to allow the development of the world in all its manifestations, tiny, emergent and boundless.

we alone have the power to usher in a new age. our forefathers and myriad Wise Beings have shown us the way—we must not get caught up in the cynicism of historical realities that belie our determination to affect change and growth.

ahh, how wondrous these magnificent words are: growth, trust, belief.
plant seeds of love with every breath, with every step, with every thought.

'taking stock'

(one of the benefits of teaching in the English system is the 6 week summer break. well earned, for we work incessantly and vigourously for 10 months of the year.)

there are myriad benefits from having a complete break from our daily routines; but also pitfalls that are to be avoided, or more to the point—faced, dealt with and overcome.

so enmeshed in our petty routines and systems in the normal run of events, it is often difficult when things come to a complete halt.

for no matter how vigilant our aspirations, routine brings with it certain blindness, a curious 'hiding away'.

this is not obvious or manifest until we STOP.

in this process, all manner of visions, appearances and realisations may surface; some welcome, others not so.

it is always surprising to me how much we (unwittingly) bury unwanted thoughts, desires and motivations in everyday life.

thus—by their very nature, subconscious thought/feelings may, worryingly, play a major part in the unfolding of our destinies in ordinary daily activity.
,
lo! the tremendous advantage and blessing of 'time out,' time to 'take stock', time to reflect deeply and unhurriedly on most recent events in our own existences.

it is in this reflective mode that much inner work can be done—i believe however, the absolute truth of the matter and using all skillful means at our disposal is to not take control of this opportunity.

we think we are in control, we think we run the show, we think we are in charge, this is unskillful positioning.

it is with the benefit of surrender, careful observance and trust that we can penetrate the heart of the matter of our existence. it is thus that i celebrate these periods of time out, as they allow the opportunity to indulge belief in the truth of this 'letting go' process.

forever vigilant, taking the open road to realisation, allowing truth to manifest without egoistic interference IS the royal road to awakening.

it is always painful to awaken to hard established habits that have become enmeshed and ingrained in our daily pursuances; it is by means of this 'taking stock mode' that we are able to establish the origin of those insidious tricks of our subconscious mind that cloud our development and keep us chained to 'samsara.'

i thank Circumstance for allowing me the chance to confront these demons and allow them to dilute, disperse and disappear in the Supreme Light of Self-awareness.

on the inside

how glorious it is to sit still.

this is truly the most wonderful skill i have learned in my life.

time and time again, life's circumstances leave me feeling lost, uptight, in a corner.

time and time again i bow, sit on my zafu (meditation cushion), offer up all my anxieties, worries, fears, screw-ups. i sit patiently whilst my mind whirls fruitlessly this way and that, looking for an explanation, looking for a 'way out.'

i find myself, like the bobsleigh rider, hanging on desperately as the train of my thoughts speeds through the labyrinths of my little consciousness and dark memories.

undeterred, i sit with all the pain, all the frustration, and all the deja-vus. i sit with faith and knowledge that these 'little self' meanderings' will eventually dissipate (i have been here endlessly before—it is just the way things work).

little self is getting impatient "come on, so many things to do; get on with it—haven't got all day etc etc."

still I sit still, holding on whilst the merry-go-round that is my mind continues to throw distraction my way; i resist the circular pull of repetition, revision and indulgence.

i have faith—i know what needs doing.

do not push anything away; just face things that arise, full on.

do not grab hold of those seductive images and ride with them, just watch them as they pass through, like the metro that rushes through the tunnel—it is not going your way.

lo and behold, THAT moment arrives.

BECOMING SUDDENLY AWAKE.

it is never the same. it is never different. it is timeless.

often i will feel tears of joy and gratitude flood out of my eyes as the mystery and beauty of the moment manifests itself.

i become aware of the coalescence of all things, the glorious light and depth of the early morning sunrise, the gentle chattering and murmur of the garden wildlife, the peacefulness of the tick/tock of the wall clock, the just-so-ness of my heartbeat, the just-as-it-is-ness of the rise and fall of my chest to the rhythms of my breathing.

i bow in the knowledge that i have learned another lesson today, now, forever:

let go of and forget your body and mind.

throw your life into the abode of awakening

living by being moved and led by the awakening of this faith in the Truth of the moment.

this is all there is, endlessly i repeat my finding.

~ with love, gratitude and homage to Great Master Dogen Zenji ~

myriad musings

this morning, whilst sitting, I was bombarded with a plethora of images and feelings from my present lifespan. this is not unusual, but, being on half-term break, I have time and space to get some of this down—call it exorcism, if you like!!

do you, like me, have a ritualistic memory? this inevitably leads to (I call it) a personality construct. In other words, we inadvertently solidify our 'self-image' by the way we access and interpret our memories. maybe this is something that becomes more entrenched, the older we get.

on some level, we have made a decision that this is how we are and each time our memory bank rolls out, we access the well-worn videos of our triumphs, disasters, almost rans, if-onlys, why-did-i-do-it—that-ways, if-only-i-had-another-go-i-would-have-done-this, etc etc ad nauseam.

this is human nature, is it not? never content with what we have, but wishing to re-write the script to suit our best version of how our lives should have run.

there is nothing wrong with having ideals, I guess, aspirations—although a lot hangs on what is the motivation behind these. now I know that, despite what is going on in my 'little self' world, there is a greater machination of which I am only dimly aware.

so, in writing this piece, I am really talking from my 'little self-world'. this is an interesting area, but ultimately, so much hot air and unworthy of over-indulgence.

I am sure there are parts of my little self biography that cause comment and may be of passing concern to others—many have said to me "you should write the story".

friends, this is far from my intention—I do not feel that my life has been worthy of mention—there are so many life stories of greatness and wonder and bravery; compared to which, my own pales into insignificance.

what I would (and do!) bang on about, time and time again is my discovery of 'abandonment'.

this is worthy of mention and may be the one thing I can share with you that will enrich and enhance your experience.

to find yourself is to lose yourself

my goodness, this is a Truth that is eternal, real and instructive.

I now know that these 'repeats' that I talked about at the beginning of this piece are so much the 'death-rattle' of my little self and, consequently, so much hot air (to put it politely).

nevertheless, they have their place and cannot be ignored—on some level it is important for us humans to contextualize our lives and our contributions to the improvement of our world.

ultimately, though, we arrive once again at the crossroads of paradox. how can we change things from this perspective? we are not Gods, mere mortals who follow life by breathing in, breathing out.

only by transparent honesty, being true, real and acknowledging our ignorance can we possibly acquit ourselves and thus be in a position to adopt our birthright of HUMANITY.

whenever we read about the lives of 'great people', and I am talking about *true* spiritual leaders here, we are struck by their humility, honesty and unfailing determination not to be swayed by little self—this is an invariable trait. this is also a barrier that each and every one of us faces when it comes down to it.

we could do well to follow examples of old masters and abandon thoughts of control and manipulation.

so, we are back to THIS.

whenever you are confronted / challenged by / with your ritualistic memories—let them pass.

our little self will always struggle for supremacy; we must be benevolent and allow it to rant and rave. one must have compassion for our little selves that attempt glorification of our little lives and let them run and run.

Only then, in time, with patience, will Truth appear, sanity and reality prevail and a sense of genuine understanding permeate our consciousness.

I implore you—do not interfere with the process, allow it to run its course, eventually you will cease to be moved or swayed by these memory apparitions and a glorious, ordinary and sanguine existence will be yours to savour.

today

today is a special day.

today I awake in harmony with Life.

today I perceive all that is before me with gratitude, joy and humility.

today I thank Divine Beings for the gift of consciousness, bodily form, understanding, discernment and the breath of life.

today I will live to the best of my ability.

today I will bow consciously at every moment—acknowledging the still, small voice that accompanies me throughout my journey.

today I will take care to regard all events with positivity, courage and warmth.

today I will be mindful to watch out for the less skillful means of my little self that fight for supremacy.

today I will respect all sentient beings and show gratitude for their teachings.

today I will forgive myself and all of humanity for our transgressions, our misunderstandings, and our failure to live up to the best of ourselves.

today I will celebrate the beauty of existence.

today I will step forward with openness of heart, freedom of mind and unwavering devotion to the wondrous panorama of universal love.

● *memoir*

a mixed bag

How affirming and 'true to form' life is.

nothing is ever simple, yet with steadfast gaze and strong heart, we can see what is true, what is real, through the murkiness of self-obsession and self-deception—we have the birthright, the sense that, leaving all attachment aside, understanding may blossom, indubitably, inexorably, unhesitatingly.

'A mixed bag' this week indeed—how the casual juxtaposition of forces manifests never ceases to amaze and inspire.

On a personal level, have been at the mercy of a wickedly virulent virus that has inhabited my body and reeked havoc with my throat, chest, stomach and mind. I have, however soldiered on through the pain and refused to be lain low.

Now for the good news . . .

something very special occurred on Thursday afternoon in my classroom;

I scarce can find words to describe the outpouring of soulfulness, love and togetherness that permeated the space there that day.

Five teenage students on the autistic spectrum; myself; my trusted assistant. There, together, a moment in time.

The theme: personal, cultural, social and health education: as you may imagine, such a coalescence of abstract ideas—as to run a line of fear through this group of boys who find theoretical discussion an anathema.

And yet and yet—I laid out the theme to them: "let's talk about our behaviour—how what we think and feel, say and do, impacts on each other."

All I can relate is that time stood still that Thursday afternoon, as my students found a magical space of uninterrupted positive good regard, and for some god-given unknown reason, SPACE and SILENCE, in which each participant was able to hold the floor with confidence and a feeling of great security and warmth.

One by one, they spoke out into the ambrosia of shared understanding and talked, deeply, intuitively, wisely, humorously, humanely about each other. These are autistic children, remember, who in the normal run of events have an emotional level way behind their peers.

You could have heard a pin drop in another galaxy for these precious sixty minutes of pure speech from these wonderfully honest and transparent lovely souls.

Myself and my assistant were close to tears with surprise and joy. We looked across at each other and time stood still with the shared knowledge of this special moment we were witness to.

Anyway, time moved on—the next hour was back to the usual 'busyness and mayhem' that is life as usual in my classroom.

But. amidst the pain of feeling physically shipwrecked I had found this oasis of wonder, briefly, finitely.

thank you Life for teasing me so deliciously.

summer's bliss

Fresh with the glow of shared company with my very beautiful, talented and intelligent seven-year-old daughter.

It is amazing how quickly a child can learn new skills—the journey from scared rookie to accomplished master is but a hair's breadth.

Ahhh! the joy of cycling down a quiet country road with my little beloved; balmy summer's afternoon, quiet hum of bees and dragonflies, smooth crunch of rubber tyres on gravel.

Watching her up front, struggling to master the art of balance and inexorably building self-confidence; eyes mist up with tears as remembrance of my own struggles half a century ago to learn similar skills, [pity I did not have such an involved and loving parent to accompany me.]

Thank the Lord for blessing me with this joy past the meridian of my days.

I wish her a long happy and fulfilled life and hope she will remember today for ever—I certainly will.

eternal moment

I was riding back home from the gym this morning, I happened to glance up at the sky.

a beautiful autumnal morning, a sky mixed with bright sunshine, scudding clouds and that perennial shading that signifies the changing season.

and then, quite simply, I 'got it'.

an overriding realisation, THIS IS IT!

this is how it is, was and will be.

In truth, this is all there is; an ordinary reflection, but in reality an extraordinary feeling of well being, belonging and, just/so/ness.

Difficult to relate and describe the joy that encompassed me. It was as if I flew instantaneously across the entire sweep of existence, from the beginning (beginning less), through myriad lifetimes, eons, until the very end (endlessness).

I saw, felt and understood everything in that moment. nothing to worry about, nothing to do, just to be.

Overriding gratitude, oceans of thanksgiving and blessings showered my path like wild, scarlet rhododendron.

I crossed over the road, entered my home for breakfast.

outpourings (or what we take for granted)

outpouring: *A pouring out, overflow; (chiefly in non-material sense and pl.) fervid expression of feelings, in words and writing.*

Last night, coming home, tired but content after a long and busy week, looking forward to spending a pleasant, light-hearted evening in with my family, waiting at the bus stop for the final link home, after walk/train/train.

what terrible provenance, what alarming synchronicity.

Only the other day I was writing my fun-poem—'A manual of digital dexterity'. This was a heart-felt prayer of gratitude and celebration for the gift of our hands, which perform endless miracles of servitude and practical self-help to all of us on a permanent basis.

Lo and behold I could not have known what vision of horror I was to face only days later.

Head immersed in thought, gathering dusk and a slight chill cascading across the dusty pavement, I happened to glance up mid-thought and recoiled in surprise, shock and horror.

This man was struggling with his mobile, trying to put it to his ear. Both his hands were . . . missing.

Both of his arms ended three-quarters of the way down from his elbows, two dark brown stumps of flesh; he had his small phone rested on the stump end and he deftly put this to his ear, using his other stump to hold the back of it, so that it would not fall. The phone kept slipping, but miraculously never fell to the ground. He kept at it, trying again and again to put it to his ear.

The cruelty of this world sometimes is beyond comprehension. This could not have been an accident, losing your hands in this way. This must have been a cynical act of violence and terror—intimidation, retribution, no doubt.

People rushing about, pretending not to notice; two ladies, moaning next to me about the lateness of the bus.

A frisson of fear and also immense admiration swept through me like wild fire . . . this guy was coping so well, so un-bothered by his plight, so 'normal.'

I tried to imagine what his life could possibly be like . . . no hands for God's sake!!

No hands, how could he do anything for himself? Imagine: brushing teeth, dressing, eating, working, writing, scratching an itch, embracing/ caressing, hailing, bowing, shaking hands, toileting, opening the door, ANY PHYSICAL ACT.

What a horror, what an affliction, yet there he was, large as life, getting on with it.

I cry inside at the unspeakable act of barbarity that caused this and the mercilessness of human action that could even think to deprive a man of his hands.

And yet, so much love beauty and compassion exists side by side.

What bravery, what courage and fortitude this person manifested at that urban bus stop at commuter hour last night.

Lest we take anything for granted, this story at least will make us grateful for the immense privilege most of us have for the gift of our limbs.

two minutes

Two minutes. this is all we are asked to give. The eleventh hour of the eleventh month.

How moving, how poignant.

Busy on my weekly domestic shopping—ensconced in my local superstore, filling my trolley with the weekly 'necessities' for my family; usual hustle and bustle, to-ings and fro-ings between aisles, making 'important' decisions—this one or that? Did we not have that last week? let me try something else etc.

An announcement across the tannoy—*'please observe two minutes silence for those who gave their lives in the two world wars, at 11am.'*

The moment arrives, gradually, imperceptibly, the whole store falls silent. within a few moments I clasp my hands together; my head drops down as I gaze absently at the contents of my shopping trolley. I can feel a monumental silence sweeping across the globe. All superficial thoughts that I held but a moment ago dissolve—instantly.

A sorrow engulfs me as a tsunami of horror and despair sweeps me from my little reality and lifts me, awesomely to a great height—from there I survey the tide of war stretching back over the panorama of human existence. The countless sacrifices of myriad innocent and brave souls bombard my conscience. My spirit contracts with misery and pain at the destitution, likewise expands with gratitude and pride at the selflessness and courage of those who paid the ultimate price for the rest of us to have the freshness and vitality of freedom.

Within this short space, an eternal moment manifests. I weep at the wonder, the grandeur and the senseless loss of life that intermingle and produce Life as we experience it. The magnificence and folly of we humans gives rise to the history of a species that, in one long breath reaches eternally to the divine and temporally succumbs to the mindlessness of greed, hatred and delusion.

I rouse myself, lift my gaze and push my trolley through to the next aisle.

a love affair with the blues

My life-long love affair with 'the Blues' sprang from a strange tangle of threads at an early age. Growing up in the UK as the eldest son of immigrant family, refugees from that Hades of a land known as Nazi Germany, I had deep within my psyche, a fear and loathing of all cultural and racial prejudice. I knew from the life story of my mother, the Armageddon of the Holocaust—she herself had fallen victim to the regime and landed up in Buchenwald, the notorious concentration camp, for the last 13 months of 'that war', finally liberated by the Americans in April '45. Emotionally and physically scarred and disfigured from this experience, Mum kept a thunderous silence on all matters pertaining to those times; only when she passed on did I discover some of her truths about this time from a secret diary she had hidden away.

Nevertheless I grew up with a strong and deep instinctual knowledge of the ferment and madness of those times; myself restricted to an austere school regime of the '50's, the world of my youth appeared a cold, forbidding place and somewhat empty of compassion. I came alive and felt some connection with the experience of Jewish cultural history that I learned about from travelling up to town on Friday evenings, to North West London, becoming ensconced in wonderfully bright and happy Sabbath meals at my Uncle and Aunt's place; they were at the centre of a thriving little community that ate, laughed and prayed together. The story of 'the Exodus' grew alive in my heart and I began to identify with the plight of the dispossessed throughout history.

Ironically my father, anxious to afford me a better start in life than he himself had encountered, sent me away to a truly English establishment which, rather than engaging me in emotional warmth that was lacking in our household, merely compounded the isolation I felt from the immigrant experience. He, however, was from a generation severely lacking in material comfort and thus his priority was the concept of financial stability—at any psychic cost. Of course, the English public school of the 50's was class-ridden and xenophobic and someone like myself, strange name, and strange customs was sure fodder for attack. I was, though, a feisty individual and prepared to defend my honour and myself at any cost and regardless of the odds.

My father had held a deep admiration and fascination for the history and values of the USA from an early age, growing up as a Jewish lad in Nazi Germany. Especially 'Westerns'—the concept of the European establishing himself in the Wild West, brought out the romance and freedom of movement that was so lacking in his own circumstance—of course we have a different slant on the annexation of the Native American by the Europeans today, but those were other times. As a consequence of his fascination and admiration for all things American, our house was littered with cultural icons of the early 20th century, fashion, art, literature, but music, especially the music: Hollywood musicals, Jazz, Country and Western and of course, Blues.

The epiphany for me was stumbling across an old, beat up vinyl LP entitled: 'Blues in the Mississippi Night'. This was a series of authentic field recordings put together by a music anthropologist called Alan Lomax, in the 1940's in the cotton fields of the Mississippi Delta. I was about 10 years old then and the experience of that first encounter stays with me to this day. Hearing those early African-American guys talking about 'life' as they encountered and experienced it, blew me away. Singing spirituals as they hacked down the cotton, incredible depth, soul, emotion in those voices, and wow!!! that rhythm . . . then, sitting down to rest and telling it 'like it was'—stories of suppression and also, for a young boy on the verge of puberty, stories of love and women. "Well, you see, the blues is like this, when a bull ain't got no cow . . ." This was pure nectar to me, an English public school boy had never encountered anything of this world before—and to be sure, the spiritual connection of suppression and downtrodden experience that I had absorbed growing up in an immigrant Jewish family—these people were my spiritual brothers!!

The icing on the cake was when some guy started singing about meeting up with his 'baby' for the Friday night dance and blowing his 'harp' (harmonica) that was it!! A lifelong long love affair with the Blues was born there and then. Not too much later, I acquired my first guitar and dedicated every waking minute to mastering the 12 bar blues structure and discovering the incredible wealth, diversity and talent of all those music masters of the Mississippi Delta and then later on the urban blues meisters of Chicago. This wonderful medium was to sustain and nourish every waking moment for the rest of my barren schooldays.

silent gossip

In moments (such as this), of extreme exhaustion and tiredness, do the glories and bones of Being reveal themselves.

The realisation of this being all there is, is stark, as plain as the deep blue sunset that pierces the gloom with magical light.
A carefree gait plays upon my spiritual frame, despite the rancour of work-related issues, the untied, loose ends, the unspoken dissatisfactions.

All these issues and frames of mind pale into insignificance as compared to the breadth, depth and import of this moment, such as it is, fleeting, casual, momentary, ephemeral, etc.
I can only let go of all attempts to control the course of events, knowing as I do, deep in my heart of hearts, that nothing really matters to a point of worrying overtly about how they may pan out.

Continuously, in the daily round, I am becoming more and more aware of the futility of trying to do, or be other than I am.
True to my self-nature, I respond as best I can, in the best way possible at each moment, to the unfolding of events, as they appear on my horizon.

I bask in the not-knowing, for I have faith that grows exponentially day by day in the power of my meditations and vows of aspiration to lead an open life.

It matters not a jot whether I succeed or fail, only that I live fully, only that I strive for awakening to each and every joyful and ghastly lump of experience that falls my way.

I do no more duck and dive, but open arms readily to the 'bliss' and the 'crap' in random order, discriminating not betwixt the two.

I no longer look for favour to the privileged ones any more than turn my back on the disenfranchised—I survey all beyond with equal credit and seek to redress imbalance created in former moments of ignorance.

An out-fashioned hippie encounters the US of A ~ fall of 1980.

This memoir I am certain is factually and chronologically correct—I remember landing at Kennedy Airport, NYC in November 1980 on my first (of two) transatlantic forays to date—it was November 4—the day the American public voted in Ronald Reagan as their new leader but, curiously, coming as it did shortly before the murder of John Lennon in New York City—my recollection is of having been in London when I heard that dreadful news—one of those puzzling inconsistencies with which I cannot square up. I am sure I spent six weeks in the States, which would have had me still Stateside at that momentous time—memory is fickle.

Preamble:

This journey I undertook was memorable in many ways—for the variety, scope, synchronicity, sheer intensity and diverse experiences I encountered along the way. It came at a time of deep unrest and confusion in my life; many years before I truly found my way. 1980 ushered in a new decade—the 70's for me had started with such promise: new uni. student in 1970, (Philosophy & Sociology—Exeter), aspirations of rock stardom (I cut a rock album in Hamburg, W Germany, 1972, produced by Uwe Nettelbeck, manager of legendary 'krautrock' band 'Faust'. This creative enterprise was cut short and finally aborted following on from the gunning down of Israelis at the Munich Olympic Games.)

For me, the 1970's were dogged by inordinately severe back luck and timing (the above is but one example of many), excruciating personal underachievement and monumentally bad life-choices. So, by the advent of 1980, I was due enrichment and a turning of the tables—the 80's however, were (personally) but a marginal improvement on the previous decade, still dogged by bad luck, lacks of sound judgment and failures on my part.

I therefore arrived in New York that fateful November, hoping for adventure and escape from uncomfortable home truths.

Itinerary:

NYC—Philadelphia—Washington DC—Richmond, Virginia—Jacksonville, Florida—Miami—Tampa, Florida—Tallahassee—Mobile, Alabama—Biloxi, Mississippi—New Orleans—Montgomery, Alabama—Atlanta, Georgia

November 4/1980—Kennedy Airport NYC

Flying across a deep blue, placid and endless Atlantic ocean, we first encountered Newfoundland, then hit the Eastern seaboard of the US on a beautiful fall afternoon—the excitement was fuelled by the anticipation of meeting long-lost old friends and also savouring the sites and sounds of history and legend—the USA!! On arrival, my first encounter was with a 'Moonie', intent on recruiting this englisher to his cause—portentous beginnings.

Now, I defy anyone not to have been thrilled and have marveled at their first encounter with the New York (Manhattan) skyline—arriving by yellow cab in the early evening, the sheer enormity of electric brilliance, overdrive and architecture was mind blowing:

I made my way up to Greenwich Village, to the studio apartment of an old uni. friend, Peter Blegvad, a musician, artist and illustrator, ('Leviathan'—the Independent), who was later to claim fame on the avant garde music scene with SlappHappy and Henry Cow. We immediately got down to playing our geetars and smoked and drank the night away with abandon, in his huge loft apartment. The next few days passed in a flurry of musical and social experiences that typified interactions of the time. (Mad, busy, mad, mad, busy . . .)

I, however, was anxious to get travelling and found a novel way of so doing. I discovered via the voluminous New York Times: 'Auto Driveaway': this was a great and novel way of travelling across the States: rich people who wanted to winter vacation in sunnier climes (e.g. Florida), also wanted their car with them, but could not be assed to drive them all that way—this is where I came in—hired drivers to take their vehicles across the continent for their use on vacation; for the price of the gasoline, I was to drive this brand-new Oldsmobile all the way down the eastern seaboard: New York to Fort Lauderdale in Southern Florida.

NYC—Richmond, Virginia

I was on my way! Armed with a brand new Oldsmobile limousine the size of a small European state, I snaked my way out of New York City, through the desperately poor neighbourhood of New Jersey:

(the unspoken of, unannounced underbelly of the US—I was shocked and appalled at the depth of poverty and squalor I encountered, adjacent as it was to the affluence of nearby NYC—dirt-littered, rubbled streets, kids running about virtually shoeless/homeless, truly a third-world scenario. This was a side of US life I was to encounter at regular intervals on my travels, especially south of the Mason-Dixon line).

So! This is it—the grand adventure begins—the wide, wide, velveteen open road ('black top'), more country music radio stations per square mile than you could shake a stick at, gasoline cheaper than water (it needed to be with a gas guzzling V8.) Driving through Philadelphia, another amazing mass of urban madness, on into Maryland, an outstanding riot of New England colours of fall—greens, purples, reds; especially yellows and browns of every nuance and shade, stunningly fecund and beautiful; scudding clouds, azure blue autumnal skies, a veritable paradise, light years away from drab London UK.

Next stop, Washington DC—in true carefree hippie style, drove right up to the White House lawn, sat there in my travelling mansion and wondered at the ease at which I was able to get so close to the corridors of supreme power. That night I drove on to Richmond, Virginia—I arrived there early evening and surprised my young, recently-relocated Mancunian brother-in-law. The reception was less than rapturous and after supper in a local diner, I ended up sleeping in the car, as he did not think his gran'mamma would be happy to see a long-haired white boy (dis-)grace her porch. The house was a ramshackle old wooden affair in a black neighbourhood and full of fascination and history for me.

Richmond, Virginia—Fort Lauderdale, Florida

Next day, I continued my journey south; I journeyed through some wonderfully American sounding towns, also revealing a rich indigenous and European heritage: Emporia, Rocky Mount, Fayetteville, Elloree, Charleston, Savannah; towards dusk, I finally passed into Florida, through Jacksonville and ended up in pitch darkness, meandering off of the main road and sleeping in the car. I awoke early next morning—in a veritable swamp! Evidence of tropical jungle, alligators and all manner of strange animals spurred me on my way.

I stopped at the aptly named Great Cove Springs for my first ever Macdonald's breakfast—this was a true innovation back in 1980 and where I encountered for the first time that weird and wonderful American invention: sausage (flat, circular) and 'hash browns' for a mere 50 cents, including eggs 'easy over' and as much coffee as I could swallow in one session.

I continued driving down the east coast of Florida throughout the day, past what was then Cape Canaveral, a forest of huge structures pointing towards the stars, until I reached my initial destination: Fort Lauderdale, just North of Miami. I dropped off the auto, in good repair, to its owners, who were renting this vast bungalow-type detached property somewhere in suburbia—all I remember is, that on entering the front door, a vast swimming pool about 25 metres in length stretching out to eternity.

I was just told, deadpan: "you can get a bus into Fort Lauderdale from across the way" and left to get on with it—uncharacteristic lack of hospitality, I felt.

I bussed it into town and was once again awestruck by the opulence and extravagance I encountered in town. The pavements were as wide as London streets in their entirety and some buildings even had deep pile red carpets outside! It was extremely hot trawling through the wide arcades. I remember an inner canal, which ran parallel to the coastal beach and was filled to the rafters with expensive and huge motor cruisers, yachts and schooners of all descriptions.

I kow-towed it to the beach and was bowled over by the beauty, temperate nature and depth of colour of the Atlantic coast this far south. I spent the night stretched out on the sand dunes and beheld a truly memorable sunrise early next morning—whew!

However—Florida was surely 'not my scene' and I decided to take a chance and head for New Orleans, Louisiana, a fair few hundred miles North and West from there. This was to prove a move of great significance for me and in narrating the story you will see provenance and synchronicity of the highest order in the subsequent unfolding of events.

Fort Lauderdale, Florida—New Orleans, Louisiana

Car hire being the ubiquitous and cheapest form of transport in those days, I hired me a bright red, shiny Chevrolet Cougar sports car for the trip to New Orleans, for next to nothing.

Needless to say, I was tickled pink to be in charge of such a piece of extravagance for my trip across Florida, (those days, easily pleased)—little did I know what was in store for me that evening.

On route from Miami toward the West coast up along the Mexican Gulf, I picked up a hitch-hiker—we drove across some esoteric indigenous American Indian reservations and swamps that day, with correspondingly exotic names: Lake Okeechobee, alongside the Caloosahatchee River, through Myakka River State Park.

It turns out that my 'companion' that day, being some sort of 'latter-day Christian evangelist', was staying at a centre, to which he invited me to spend the night. Little did I know what I had let myself in for. We pulled off the road, just south of Tampa and entered this 'nether world' the like of which I had never imagined possible and to which I subsequently vowed never, ever to return as long as I had breath in my body. Consisting mainly of mobile homes, I was ushered into these folks' home and then subjected to a form of right-wing racist propaganda that had me quaking in my boots. Why I just did not turn tail immediately and head outta there I do not know (too scared, I think.)

Anyway, it turns out that these folks were convinced that "Satan had arrived in the USA as a black lesbian and all black folk the reason for all that ailed the 'glorious Amurican Reepublic'." What would they do to me if they knew I was married to an African American and father to two bi-racial children? Needless to say, I kept real quiet about that.

Later that evening I was subjected to a gathering of similar-minded maniacs in a huge purpose built dome and had to endure a couple of hours of mindless proselytizing by some jerk preacher, his adoring congregation jumping up in unison every two minutes shrieking: "HALLELIUH, PRAISE THE LORD!!"

I spent what was probably the most uncomfortable night of my life in these folks' home and could not wait to escape the next morning—whew!

Driving northwest up the gulf with a huge sense of relief and feeling of having escaped death by insanity, I eventually cut out of Florida and passed through Mobile Alabama, a temperate wasteland and shortly into the exotically named, Biloxi, Mississippi. Toward evening, I prepared to enter New Orleans with great expectation. The arrival was truly awe inspiring:

To reach New Orleans from the east by road, you have to cross Lake Pontchartrain via a 5 or 10—mile long bridge that hugs the water all the way across.

The view of the city of New Orleans at sunset, approaching it from the lake, was simply stunning and remains eternally etched upon my memory.

New Orleans & R.T.P.:

Now, I can reveal one of the most synchronous and strange happenstances that I encountered in my whole life; to rewind an instant: way back in 1967, when I was a 15-year-old public-school boy whose horizons were entirely filled with girls and blues music, both in the hearing, listening and playing, I met a young guy from the Lake District in Northern England who was to have a profound effect on my life.

The circumstances were somewhat convoluted. One of my best friends at school, J. B., (with whom I played in a Blues Band—Tearman's Blues Band), having already left school that year, being some two academic years ahead of me (God how we envied him!) had travelled 'up North' and was living in a border town called Carlisle, on the Scottish frontier—this barren and windswept town was a full day's hike from London. Come the winter holiday, I lost no time in hitching a ride up there to see him.

There they were, the two of them, living an adult life—earning real good money, working on the newly built M6 motorway, playing music at every spare moment, romancing girls and enjoying life to the fullest. R. cut a dashing figure in those days, young, raven-haired, great looking, cutting a dash with the local young women and with an irrepressible humor and an indefatigable energy for all the good things in life. At 18, he had all the charisma of eternal youth and a bravado and zest that seemed truly monumental. A hero, a role model to a young impressionable school kid like me!

Over the next few years our friendship grew; later, he disappeared to the States when I was just setting up shop in London, trying to get a foothold in the music business. He came back, in a whirlwind as usual, recently married to beautiful young American-Armenian lass, whom he had met whilst becoming a New Orleans street musician. His adopted family had afforded them a six-month European honeymoon. Boy, had he landed on his feet there! The girl came from a wealthy family and later was to set him up with a famous and culturally historic recording studio in Bristol City, Tennessee.

We spent the summer months playing and partying every weekend in his little North London pied-a-terre at the base of Alexandra Palace—it was dreamy and fun. He then left to return stateside and I was not to see him again until my descent into New Orleans, some 8 years later. Now, I had completely fallen out of touch with him—all I knew was that, 8 years previously, he had returned to New Orleans with his new bride—I had heard nada—nothing during that time.

So, I was taking a huge gamble, a long-shot, if ever there was one, in expecting to find him so many years later in a big city.

Cutting back to the trip—just crossed Lake Pontchartrain on that glorious autumnal evening—I headed into town—where to start looking? I made for the French quarter, which is where all the music happens and seemed like the obvious first port of call.

I parked up, and headed into a bar—the first one that came to hand. There was a band playing on stage—this crazed, hunched-back one-legged singer was belting out a Jackson Brown number—I did a round turn, staggered and almost lost it—it was him!! R., my old buddy, up there as usual, wildly entertaining the crowd.

But how he had changed—I scarcely recognized him; gaunt, wasting away, minus one leg, he was but the vaguest shadow of his former self. Wow, when the number finished and I ran up to the stage, it was if time stood still—that reunion remains one of the most potent and emotional moments of my life. Of course, I had to join the band up there that night and we played a rip-roaring set that had the punters on their feet.

However, once the joy and excitement had worn away, I realize that my buddy was really in a desperate and hellish situation—things had gone extremely awry for him in the intervening years—he had lost his right leg below the knee in a motorbike accident, had ended up in the infamous House of the Rising Sun'—a Louisianan penitentiary and now was a virtually starving and impecunious street musician, living solely on his wits—separated from his lovely wife at the time and living in some rat-infested garret in the poorest part of town. I did what I could for him, but selfishly, had plans to visit another buddy who was up in Atlanta, Georgia—I hung around with R. for a few days, but left him, to drive the few hundred miles upstate to Atlanta—I gave him as much money as I could spare and vowed to revisit him at a later date—the parting was fraught, he begged me not to leave and I did so with a bad taste in my mouth.

Atlanta, Georgia—Julian (& J.)

At last; arriving in beautiful, sun filled, leafy suburban Atlanta was a wonderful moment—not least as it betokened a joyful and warm reunion with two of my greatest buddies form Exeter uni. days:—Julian Brogi and J. G., a wonderful couple of erudite and beautiful souls from Ealing in West London; our friendship had been, instant, deep and spontaneous from the very first meeting—kindred spirits in the world of literature, art and music, this bonded couple (the 'perfect couple' if there ever was such a thing,) both heralded from immigrant families, as do I—Julian, half English, half-Italian, J., half—French, half English. We spent two glorious years as friends, going everywhere together, doing everything together—like a close knit family of compadres. They had acquired the archetypal VW camper van, so ubiquitous of the sixties and seventies, with a miniscule engine with a top speed way in excess of 20 miles per hour!

Alas, even their impeccable togetherness had been eroded by their move over to Georgia—they were, much to my amazement, no longer a couple when I arrived, but still good friends and colleagues—how times change the unchangeable! There I was, happily ensconced in suburban leafy, Atlanta.

Julian, (Ju), was part of an up and coming rock outfit that was beginning to establish a name for itself state wide. At uni, and thereafter in London, we had played frequently in bands together—Ju was an amazing drummer and, I, as guitarist without compare (in Notting Hill Gate, at least,) our playing had a spark and intensity of great proportion and depth—imagine if you will, a youthful John McLaughlin and Billy Cobham, such was the nature of our interactive musical expression.

So, I passed several glorious and fun-filled weeks in Atlanta—venturing downtown, to historic sites as Martin Luther King Boulevard and catching the latest wow movie in town—the Elephant Man, with John Hurt. I became Ju's chauffeur whilst in town, driving around in his beat up 1950's V6 monster.

I befriended a young lady who was an Americana collector and we spent several weekends checking out Americana fairs in and around Atlanta—we had a ball and later I persuaded her to drive down with me, back to New Orleans to check up on Richard—this was an unmitigated disaster, as upon arrival, I was piggy-in-the-middle between a needy old friend and an even needier new girlfriend.

Not being able to satisfy either of their needs to their satisfaction, I was forced to retreat back to Atlanta, as T. needed to get back to work. On the way back, we stopped off at a motel in Montgomery, Alabama—site of not too distant race riots—a vey heavy and foreboding place indeed. As luck would have it, T's auto engine blew up 50 miles outside of Atlanta and we had to bus it back—an inauspicious end to a fatefully flawed voyage.

I had by now run out of funds and in typically American eighties style I stumbled on a couple of way-off-the-peg employment opportunities:

1. Extra in Canadian movie: 'Hard Feelings'—this was an anti—war movie about a young Canadian draft dodger—whilst on the run in Atlanta, I was hired to play the part of, of all things an American G.I.!! Kitted out in full, authentic G.I. uniform, including dog tag, I strode around Atlanta like a true American Boy. On meeting me, the director, hearing my English accent, commented: "Whatever you do, do not open your goddarn mouth!" I spent 3 days filming/sitting on an unmoving greyhound bus—payment $100 a day, plus all I could eat—nice work if you can get it!

2. Shelf builder for a shoe designer in a shopping mall: This lasted just a few hours—payment: $50.

Thus ended my truly memorable transatlantic jaunt—a couple of days later I took off from Atlanta airport on a Delta Airlines flight to Heathrow, watch out for next visit in 1999—cutting CDs and laying old ghosts to rest.

- *philosophical reflection*

ten degrees of separation

Dukka / suffering / dissatisfaction / dissociation / disquiet / dislocation / dis-ease.

so many and more intricate and subtle words describing separation.

Is it any wonder that we struggle so? For we have become disconnected by virtue of our situation, our existential condition.
Given this 'body, mind and consciousness', nurtured (or not as is often the case) to an equivalent maturity, we are not shown the essence, the 'élan vital', the vital step to awakening from the little mind understanding [its whereabouts] to an awakening that belies our initial framework and perspective.

All too often we are taught that illumination, worthiness, morality is just beyond our grasp. Never are we shown that, here and now, this is IT, nowhere else to go, nothing else to achieve; awakening is this. This is all there is.

This is rude awakening.

This is the Truth.

We can like it or lump it, for sure. We often lump it. This is okay.

Moreover, the initial trip from birth to self-consciousness is a fall from Grace.

An awesome unity propels us into the open arms of earthly existence from the internal embrace of our maternal transport machine ~ from this point on, it is stumble, trip, descend, stumble trip descend until, arriving at that independence of puberty, we inherit the persona of 'self-direction'.

Naturally, this period is one of immense arrogance as we cruise through the unbidden social confines and feel ourselves immortal.

Then and only when we have reached the barrier, the wall of discontent and bewilderment do we give pause. When a reality shakes us out of our liberal blindness and, bemused, we lower our gaze, shake our heads mournfully, and take in the scrabble of mundanity, only then, when all options of escape are used up, not until then do we have the opportunity ~ thrust upon us, to truly get to grips with this performance.

Cast off this illusory pretence of knowledge!!

Fear not the gulf of misunderstanding!!

Be not afraid to cast off body mind and soul and jump whole heartedly into the abyss of the present moment.

For wherever you may arrive, it is only a leap of Faith that holds you in tender embrace and comforts you.

The truth will heal you, the not-knowing, the fear terror and disbelief would melt and conjoin you with the absolute.

Never again need you fret. You will fret, you will feel pain, you will hurt, and you will suffer.

But it is a different quality of being.

For with this honest surrender of will, comes unity. Never again need you wonder why. Never again will you need to prepare, rearrange, and put on a show.

For you have accepted the Truth and it will forever hold you as one with the breath of That Which Is.

Zero degrees of separation now entitle you to a life of joy, bliss and happiness. Banish those thoughts of victory, dispel images of understanding. Hold yourself high and open your arms to the mystery and wonder that lie patiently awaiting your coalescence.

blessed

blessed with human form, abilities to gain insight by skilful application of opening to 'It.'

despite the social and cultural conditioning that imprints our worldly perception from an early age, it is indeed possible to break the bonds of mental reasoning.

if only we give full credence to our innate ability to settle into a timeless and formless state of being, then with faith we reach satisfaction, peace and tranquility.

we live, we move, we change, we grow.

we must form choiceless acceptance of the moment as it manifests; we come to understand and appreciate that our limited will cannot inform the Greater Passage.

we emerge, shy, blinkered, shielding our view to gain insight; in awe, non-believing in such simplicity.

(reculer pour mieux sauter.)

laughter is kept in check—we cannot believe our good fortune; we are in shock—this cannot be so easy; this cannot be so effortless—freedom—freedom from desire, freedom from fear, freedom from . . . yes, ourselves.

delight, gratitude, ecstasy, liberation from lifelong bondage to little self and all the baggage.

emptiness, of the fullest sort—space, light, fluidity, indescribable energy, effortless joy, pleasure-less sympathy and coalescence—manifest beyond any explicable realm, beyond any rational description.

and then, change:

the darkness of samsara envelops our awakening and dis-belief renders us wordless and shaken.

learning to let go, we enable blessedness to drain into our yearning for perfection and learn the hard lessons of changeable-ness.

we acknowledge the moment, yet again, and again the passage of fortune shifts and reappears in unrecognizable form.

perfection is not for us. perfection is not of us. excellence of passage however is our fundamental birthright and it is this striving for the best we can possibly do that unleashes our potential.

we were, are and will be forever blessed with this miracle of puzzlement and fortuitous awareness.

with bows.

This piece of writing was written 'around the late eighties' whilst I was supervising a bunch West London 'inner city kids' on a boat on the Norfolk Broads, and kind of sums up my views on life, the universe and everything at that point in my life:

cycle / I am

"That's it! That's really it!!"
At last, the final bend, out of the darkness, the goal is in sight . . .

It is hard to describe and many would say, ultimately futile to attempt so to do—the moment of Final Illumination, the turning of the key that finally unlocks the door of Illusion, but here I am forced to attempt it, so, gentle reader, I present my case:

* Pleasing as an Aid to the Mind's digestion is the application of FORM and STRUCTURE to the essential FORMLESSNESS and STRUCTURE FREE reality, which we confront, vying for the cutting edge, and tremulously taking the 'élan vital', the ESSENTIAL step to BEING.

(The truth is that it is futile to try to shut out the world—many cultural traditions espouse the ideal of the hermit's path to self-enlightenment.)

What road leads to this all embracing loneliness? It is a journey. But a journey that becomes the reality that it is. The travelers on this journey are you, the world, time and space. Where is the centre? You, you are the centre. I, I am the centre. We, we are the centre. Who am I? Who are you? We are the centres. We are alone, together. Together, alone. You are in my thoughts sometimes. Sometimes You are with me. I am in my thoughts sometimes. I am with me. When I'm with me, sometimes I am kind to myself and sometimes I am hard on myself.

Still, I endure.

And in enduring I learn to live. For we are all learning to live, all the time. Even when we're not learning, we're learning. Even though we are not sleeping, we are sleeping. Even though we are not awake, WE are awake.

We are unaware that we are aware . . .

The list is endless.
(The list is to port/starboard*)

[*Delete as appropriate]

To come round endlessly to the point is the hellish walk round the Eternal Bend that is ego trying to control personal existence.

This is the kernel, the bit that is hard to swallow, and the unreachable centre that will not crack under any pressure, which will retain Integrity and Form.
Enter the centre.

Swallow the unswallowable. Be brave, be warrior-like. Be not afraid. As a fellow traveler who travels that path. I offer reassurance. It is nothing to fear, for in the Stillness, Integrity stays with you, your reflection on and of the Form crystallizes and hence energizes your Integral Self.
Your surrender is automatic, complete. Your acceptance is Total, Abstract. Piece by piece, the myriad parts of the Whole gel together, fuse, yet Awareness remains aloof. Awareness treads the cautious path between Inner Certainty and Outer Absorption. Like a current, Awareness travels both hither and thither, tracing a discernable path, yet strangely growing (dissipating simultaneously).

Feed, feed. Constantly. Feed on growth, feed on the flow. Learn to flow, learn to open.

Openness of heart leads to vulnerability. Self-love protects the unprotected centre. But there is more, much more to come.

Nothing will be left out. For there will be nothing left. Something exists because nothing doesn't. The mind, language, communication, thoughts, ideas, images, emotions, physical ailments, pleasurable bodily sensations, and encounters—all these things play a part in connecting the self/you/me to the world.

The eternal triangle:-

Being

Self   World

The eternal dichotomy / duality

Being—Not Being
The eternal dichotomy / duality
Being—Not Being

penultimate dimension

●

the dot

the centering,

reaching the hub.

The metaphysics:

beyond the physical,

beyond the facts.

above and behind,

below and on each side

ultimate dimension.

Beyond dimension and so confusing rationality.

I am.

I am trying hard to describe BEING.

I am succeeding / failing*

[delete as appropriate*]

I am satisfied.

I am.

"That's it! That's really it!!"
At last, the final bend, out of the darkness, the goal is in sight . . .

~ epilogue ~

siafu unframed

raising my head upward,
I averted downturned gaze,
fresh from surveying
grimy sidewalk.

peace unbridled, iridescent calm,
boundaries dissolved,
I awoke.

and so, gradually, my glance became steady,
the light brightened, unnoticed.
my thoughts diffused, imperceptibly,
I no longer inhabited 'self','
the picture lost its edges:
I breathed in the universe.

I became aware of a greater notion,
my heart-place swelled with joy,
happily relinquishing the power to
influence proceedings.

no fear dwelt there, a living,
nectarine Presence suffused the air,
no inhibition, no misunderstanding—
absolute communion.

peace unbridled, iridescent calm,
boundaries dissolved,
I awoke.

I knew then, that indiscriminate opening
of heart and mind was the key to
wisdom and understanding.

there was no thing to fear save fear itself ~
ugliness, judgment and bearing pain
became historic illusion:
there was only rampant awareness
and indescribable beauty.

peace unbridled, iridescent calm,
boundaries dissolved,
I awoke.

Lightning Source UK Ltd.
Milton Keynes UK
UKOW04f0709120116

266203UK00002B/226/P